# Job Search Rescue
## 100 Strategies on How to Get Unstuck

Greg Fall

Also the author of *You, On Paper: Expert Help on How to Write a Resume*

Core Choices Publishing

Katy Harkleroad, Editor

**Job Search Rescue: 101 Strategies on How to Get Unstuck**

Copyright © 2014 by Greg Fall

All rights reserved. Without prior written permission of the author, absolutely no part of this book may be copied, reproduced, stored electronically in a database or retrieval system, recorded, transmitted, or distributed in form and/or via any means.

The publisher and author, while using best efforts, make no representations or warranties as to the accuracy or thoroughness of this book and disclaim any implied warranties. No warrantee may be created by sales agents. The counsel and advice contained in this book may not apply or be suitable to your situation. Neither the publisher nor the author shall be liable for any profit, loss, or commercial damages whether incidental, consequential, or other.

All resumes and other supporting materials have either been created by the author or have been freely allowed by others. All names utilized in this book on the sample resumes and other documents or in the context of illustrating learning points have been manufactured by the author and do not represent actual individuals. All illustrations, stories, and examples in the book are the creation of the author from many thousands of observations over 15+ years of career work and, again, do not specifically represent actual individuals.

*Cover Design by Katy Harkleroad*

Core Choices Publishing

ISBN 978-0-9960988-1-6

Fall, Greg
Job search rescue: 100 strategies on how to get unstuck
    Includes index
    ISBN: 978-0-9960988-1-6
    1. Authorship. 2. Job Hunting.

**Sincere appreciation...**

For the thousands of clients who have been my teachers over the past 15+ years. You have helped me develop a deep well of expertise and greater compassion to be able to make a difference in the lives of other job seekers.

For Katy Harkleroad, a talented editor, proofreader, and artist who continues to increase the usability of my jungly work. You make it easy to work with you, are committed to client satisfaction, remain open to learning, are generous with well developed ideas, and seek to make a difference in the lives of others. I greatly value our collaborations.

For my immediate family of Joy, Alice, and Earl. You each and all support my work to help others, even when it impacts our time together.

For God and the energy of the universe. Even as I continue to work on my human limitations, you have chosen to give me gifts, guidance, and confidence in my own journey so that I might help others in their journeys.

# Table of Contents

| | |
|---|---|
| Introduction | xi |
| Editor's Note | xv |
| **Chapter 1:  Reboot** | **1** |
| *10 Job Search Essentials* | *2* |
| *What Worked and What Didn't* | *4* |
| *SWOT Analysis* | *5* |
| *10 Getting Started Essentials* | *6* |
| **Chapter 2:  Eliminate Distractions** | **9** |
| *Strategy #1: Stop the Screen Sucking* | *10* |
| *Strategy #2: Leave Home: Three Options* | *11* |
| *Strategy #3: Ditch the Phone* | *12* |
| *Strategy #4: Pretend You are Paying Yourself* | *13* |
| *Strategy #5: Set Hourly or 15-Minute Mini-Goals* | *13* |
| *Strategy #6: Schedule Five Minute Stretch Breaks* | *14* |
| *Strategy #7: Take Spontaneous Breaks* | *14* |
| *Strategy #8: Consult a Guru* | *15* |
| **Chapter 3:  Network Smarter** | **17** |
| *Strategy #9: Contact Competitors Who Defeated You* | *18* |
| *Strategy #10: Start Your Own Networking Group* | *19* |
| *Strategy #11: Network with Past Interviewers* | *20* |
| *Strategy #12: Reach Out to Junior Level Contacts* | *20* |
| *Strategy #13: Connect Back to College* | *21* |
| *Strategy #14: <u>Don't</u> Ask if Contacts Know of Openings* | *22* |
| *Strategy #15: Give a Gift to a Networking Contact* | *23* |
| *Strategy #16: Identify 10+ New Target Companies* | *24* |
| *Strategy #17: Re-Network with Former Contacts* | *26* |
| *Strategy #18: Make Networking Goals an Absolute* | *27* |
| *Strategy #19: Try These 25 Networking Quick-Hitters* | *27* |

## Chapter 4: Power Up Your Resume  31

*Strategy #20: Add a Tagline/Brand Statement*  32
*Strategy #21: Customize with a Functional Title*  33
*Strategy #22: Prominently Place Hard Skills*  33
*Strategy #23: Showcase 2-3 Core Strengths*  34
*Strategy #24: Customize Core Strengths*  35
*Strategy #25: Add Numbers*  36
*Strategy #26: Include Testimonials*  37
*Strategy #27: Use T-Style or Bullet Style Cover Letters*  38
*Strategy #28: Use a Targeted Reference List*  39
*Strategy #29: Create Addendums*  40
*Strategy #30: Try These 15 Tips for Using the Resume*  41
*Strategy #31: Hire a Professional*  44

## Chapter 5: Take Action  47

*Strategy #32: Speak with Your Actions*  49
*Strategy #33: Do Your Best*  49
*Strategy #34: Push Your Shoulders Back*  50
*Strategy #35: Create Your Own Luck*  50
*Strategy #36: Let Your Light Out*  51
*Strategy #37: Act Great*  51
*Strategy #38: Don't Fight Your Fears*  52
*Strategy #39: Access Additional Resources*  52

## Chapter 6: Acquire Hard Skills  55

*Strategy #40: Know What Skills the Market Wants*  57
*Strategy #41: Explore Various Training Options*  58
*Strategy #42: Acquire a Certification*  59

## Chapter 7: Change  61

*Strategy #43: Listen Openly to Gain New Insight*  63
*Strategy #44: Ask for Advice*  63
*Strategy #45: Do the Opposite*  64
*Strategy #46: Unplug*  64
*Strategy #47: Simplify*  65

## Chapter 8: Embrace Social Media — 67

*Strategy #48: Manage Your Digital Reputation* — 68
*Strategy #49: Update Your LinkedIn Profile* — 68
*Strategy #50: Be Active in Three LinkedIn Groups* — 69
*Strategy #51: Send a Consistent Message* — 69
*Strategy #52: Contact Recruiters via Groups* — 70
*Strategy #53: Add Recruiters as Connections* — 71
*Strategy #54: Reverse-Engineer Social Media Contacts* — 71
*Strategy #55: Find Recruiters via Your Contacts* — 71
*Strategy #56: Leverage Facebook* — 72
*Strategy #57: Tweet Your Way to a Job* — 73

## Chapter 9: Write — 75

*Strategy #58: Blog* — 76
*Strategy #59: Develop White Papers* — 77
*Strategy #60: Post Links to Articles on LinkedIn* — 78
*Strategy #61: Send Writings to the Hiring Manager* — 79
*Strategy #62: Interview the Hiring Manager* — 80
*Strategy #63: Write a Market Review of a Company* — 81
*Strategy #64: Create a 30-60-90 Plan* — 82
*Strategy #65: Write a Letter to the CEO* — 83

## Chapter 10: Boost Confidence — 85

*Strategy #66: Schedule Quick Confidence Boosters* — 86
*Strategy #67: Turn Weaknesses into Strengths* — 87
*Strategy #68: Ask Others to Boost Your Spirits* — 87
*Strategy #69: Use Your Professional Strengths* — 88

## Chapter 11: Take a Team Approach — 91

*Strategy #70: Recruit a Job Search Team* — 92
*Strategy #71: Assemble a Resume Review Team* — 92
*Strategy #72: Team Up with Salespersons* — 93
*Strategy #73: Organize a Resume Blitz* — 93
*Strategy #74: Recruit a Truth Team for Big Changes* — 94
*Strategy #75: Recruit an Accountability Buddy* — 94

## Chapter 12: Talk the Talk — 97

*Strategy #76: Record Yourself* — 98
*Strategy #77: Attend Group Meetings* — 98
*Strategy #78: Read a "How to" Book* — 99
*Strategy #79: Volunteer in a Sales Role* — 99
*Strategy #80: Join a Toastmasters Group* — 99

## Chapter 13: Go Where You're Trusted — 101

*Strategy #81: Contact Former Employers* — 102
*Strategy #82: Contact Competitor Companies* — 102
*Strategy #83: Contact Former Co-workers* — 103

## Chapter 14: Make Better Decisions — 105

*Strategy #84: Decide to Decide* — 106
*Strategy #85: Be Bold; Lead Yourself* — 107
*Strategy #86: Resolve Conflict by the Situation* — 107
*Strategy #87: Use Decision-Making by Quadrant* — 108
*Strategy #88: Consider Intent v. Impact* — 109
*Strategy #89: Think AND Feel* — 109
*Strategy #90: Use Pull-Pull Instead of Balance Sheet* — 110
*Strategy #91: Talk with Others to Gain Clarity* — 110
*Strategy #92: Separate Needs from Wants* — 111
*Strategy #93: Know When to Call in the Calvary* — 111

## Chapter 15: Re-Introduce Yourself — 113

*Strategy #94: Don't Be Defensive* — 114
*Strategy #95: Don't Show Shame or Guilt* — 114
*Strategy #96: Be the Comeback Kid* — 115
*Strategy #97: Don't Apologize* — 115
*Strategy #98: Show What You Have Been Doing* — 116
*Strategy #99: Send Out a Revised Resume* — 117
*Strategy #100: Demonstrate Your New Approach* — 117
*Strategy #101: Be Your Best Self* — 118

## Bonus Chapter: Six Lists of Top 10 Tips — 121

## Selected Resources — 135

# Introduction

It's time for a job search do-over.

Chances are you already know that, since you are reading this. That's a good sign. Because it means you are ready to: learn from past mistakes, get help, re-tool, re-energize, and re-start your job search.

Don't hide your head in shame or furrow your brow in frustration. There is nothing wrong with do-overs. Life is full of them.

Probably a third of the more than 8,000 individuals I have trained and coached in job search techniques were re-starting stalled efforts when I met them. Additionally, I have also had to re-energize my *own* career from time to time. So give yourself a break about the past; learn from it and move forward.

Just make sure that, going forward, you get it right. Because the market is unforgiving. And, no matter what the unemployment rate is, "living wage" jobs will be scarce and competitively sought after for some time. The bottom line?

**<u>There are no shortcuts</u>**. No easy answers. Not in this book. Not in any book that speaks the truth.

So, do the work. Believe in yourself. Get the right answers to the right questions. And make good decisions. This book will help you do just that!

## Know what this book "is" and "is not."

This book assumes that you have a resume and understand the basics of job searching because you have done it before (after all, this is a job search rescue). Just in case you're a little rusty on the basics, however, I'll start you out as gently as I can with a "reboot" of sorts in the first chapter. I'll also provide you with some reminders of how to stay on task. An additional bonus chapter at the end of the book offers six quick-hitter "Top 10 Tips" lists, covering:

- Revising the Resume
- Applying for a Job
- Daily Job Search
- Networking
- Interviewing
- Negotiating

These 60 quick-hitter "bonus" tips aren't included in the book's 101 strategies. I just know that some of the strategies in this book are pretty heavy-duty so you may need to revisit the basics now and then.

Also, since this book is focused on getting you back into job search mode in order for you to get noticed and secure an interview, <u>it does include strategies for topics such as resume revision and networking, but it does not dive into what happens once you are able to secure an interview.</u>

If I had chosen to get into interviewing, negotiating, onboarding, and other areas, the book's content would be much longer than the current 133 pages and it would start to become more of a comprehensive job search book and less of a "pocket guide."

Certainly, however, I would strongly encourage you to seek additional help with interview preparation and strategy well in advance of getting the call to meet with the hiring manager.

## My intent and writing style.

As this book is meant to be a "pocket guide" of sorts, its pages and strategies have been designed for ease of reference. I have concentrated on giving you powerful content in a highly usable form.

However, since this book is *not* all-inclusive, please expect that you'll occasionally need to research certain concepts more extensively (via the web or other sources) in order to gain a greater understanding of them before you execute.

While my editor, Katy Harkleroad, has helped make these strategies easier for you to comprehend, I might still offer more detail on certain points than you feel necessary. Just remember, <u>you get one chance at this</u> — and you don't want to find out, down the road, that you forgot an important detail.

So digest as much as you can.

## This book is a reference tool.

This book is intended for you to be able to pick it up, open to a page, and find a useful strategy, without having to read the previous 50 pages. The ideas and concepts in this book can be used together or separately.

As you will notice, *the strategies are organized by chapter, so that you may quickly refer to a section of interest.* I would still recommend reading the entire book, however. You will find greater help when you consider the strategies as a whole. In addition, even if you don't think you'll ever read certain chapters, I suggest quickly perusing every one before you dig into content of greatest interest. You don't want to find out that you could have, in fact, benefited from certain strategies after it's too late.

## Tough love is on the way.

This book can be your lifeline of sorts, to help bring a bit of light to the dark places in which you might find yourself. But, some of this won't be easy to hear or implement.

*And you are the one who has to do the implementing!*

So, dig in and go rescue your job search!

With sincere best wishes and positive regard,

Greg

# Editor's Note

An author is not so different from a master explorer who is blazing a trail through uncharted land. And the editor is, therefore, the author's one-person trail crew. So, while the author expertly picks the final destination and the best route of travel, it is the editor who must ensure that those who follow — the readers — can do so comfortably and safely.

In the case of this book, Greg wants you to scale a pretty lofty peak — getting your stalled job search back on track. But in getting to the apex, he takes you through some dense, jungly terrain that, at times, can be unpleasant and even difficult for you to confront. It has been my goal as Greg's editor, therefore, to judiciously prune, chop, level, and build so that you can safely move through the challenging bookscape in order to reach the summit and, ultimately, get noticed and get hired.

Keep this trail guide in your pocket, refer to it often, and mark it up liberally — customizing it for your own, unique job-search rescue.

Best Wishes on Your Trek,

Katy Harkleroad

# Chapter 1

## Reboot

Review job search fundamentals to help you evaluate your past efforts and prepare to restart your job search.

*"The way to get started is to quit talking and start doing."*
- Walt Disney

Before we get started, I want to acknowledge that I *do* understand that this whole job search redux might feel a bit overwhelming or even unpleasant at times.

My advice may sometimes come across as less than forgiving but it is offered with heartfelt hope that you will be able to improve your employment situation. If you get overwhelmed, just focus on putting one foot in front of the other. Before you know it, you will have taken the steps needed to get your job search back on track.

While this book assumes you understand and have been working at all aspects of job search, let's briefly review 10 job-search fundamentals and a couple other tools to help you identify what has worked in the past and what needs fixing. Then, after our Chapter 1 reboot, we'll dig into the first job search rescue strategies in Chapter 2.

## 10 Job Search Fundamentals

### 1. Create Top Quality Written Materials

In an era of resume "grade inflation," your resume, LinkedIn and other social media profiles, reference list, cover letters, and any other written material better be "A+" quality. They must clearly state a compelling value proposition and be mistake-free.

### 2. Focus on Networking as 75% of Your Activity

There is no substitute for phone or in-person contact. You must be networking 20+ hours per week. Simply hiding behind that screen and submitting applications online goes nowhere.

### 3. Target Hiring Managers

I have great respect for HR, but they can't help you. Your resume must get to the hiring manager and show how you can take away or prevent their pain. *Their perception is their reality.*

### 4. Create a Team

A successful job search almost always involves references, advisors, resume proof-readers, and networking contacts.

### 5. Be Authentic AND Credible

You must show both your true self and your professional self. It is critical to be "real" while simultaneously marketing/selling your ability to get results.

### 6. Take Care of Yourself

From working with thousands of clients, I can attest that this might be the biggest factor in landing a good job sooner. You must take care of your own needs in areas such as: nutrition, emotional and spiritual connection, exercise, and feeling valued.

### 7. Develop 10–20 Example Stories

You gain credibility by demonstrating to others *how you get results*. Whether in networking, on your resume, or in the interview, these example stories are critical.

### 8. Choose to Take Responsibility

Take responsibility for controlling everything you can. And let go of everything you can't. Don't blame the market for poor execution but be smart enough to listen to its messages.

### 9. Develop Achievable Goals and Specific Plans

It is prudent to pursue and regularly review both Plan A and Plan B, each with measurable objectives, action steps, and timelines. Having 10+ target companies for each plan is a must.

### 10. Never Give Up

Reboot as often as required, letting go of ego and pride while confidently embracing openness and continuous learning. Change strategies and focus on the present. All you should expect at any moment is your best.

So, how have your past job search efforts measured up against my list of job search fundamentals?

## What Worked and What Didn't

You cannot afford to repeat the mistakes of the past. Nor can you afford to forget or jettison what has worked for you in the past.

ACTIVITY: Keeping the book open to the "10 Job Search Fundamentals" pages, brainstorm two lists: one representing the strategies that worked for you in the past (e.g. effective resume, networking with former co-workers, using LinkedIn, etc.) and another list representing the strategies that didn't work so well for you in the past (e.g. staying at home in front of a computer screen, complaining about the market, procrastinating, etc.). Then, force your ego to take a vacation by sharing the lists with a trusted friend, asking for their honest yet empathetic input. Once you believe the lists to be complete, post them where they can serve as daily reminders.

Other critical questions you might ask yourself: Should I better understand and apply the basics before I learn new strategies for rebooting my search? Did I allot enough time for weekly job search tasks? Are there external factors, such as geography, that present overwhelmingly negative influences? Are my goals realistic?

# SWOT Analysis

Perform a SWOT analysis to more accurately assess your present situation before moving forward. SWOT—**S**trengths, **W**eaknesses, **O**pportunities, and **T**hreats—is a tried-and-tested method used by businesses to assess their prospects for success. It can also be helpful to you by providing an understandable framework for considering your own job search situation. In a SWOT analysis, "S" and "W" relate to internals (you) and "O" and "T" relate to externals (the market).

ACTIVITY: One way you might develop a SWOT analysis is to ask three or four trusted advisors to each spend 10–15 minutes creating—from their own perspective—four separate lists for the *strengths, weaknesses, opportunities,* and *threats* they perceive to be relevant to your search. In other words, you would ask each person to give you feedback on your professional strengths and weaknesses, as well as on market opportunities and threats. You should also brainstorm your own list. Then, compare the lists to better validate some of your own thoughts and correct or add in additional items.

Finished with the SWOT analysis? Before we move on to the 101 job search rescue strategies, let's do one last review. The following is a list of 10 essentials for getting started on your effort to reboot your stalled job search.

## 10 Getting Started Essentials

### 1. Revise Resume and Marketing Materials

These don't have to look completely different from earlier versions, but find ways to increase the resume's effectiveness. State your value clearly and back it up with concrete examples. That will signal you are ready for prime time.

### 2. Revise or Create a LinkedIn Profile

LinkedIn is, essentially, your online resume. In today's market, not having a fully populated profile raises questions related to transparency and whether you have embraced the digital age. Plus, LinkedIn is an indispensable networking tool for your search. Smile in that headshot!

### 3. Revise or Create Lists of Target Companies

A "rolling" list of 10+ companies each for Plan A and Plan B helps you target your networking and stay on task. Adjust the lists as necessary.

### 4. Revise or Create an Effective Elevator Pitch

Your 30–60 second intro can't be delivered in monologue, except at certain formal networking events. Use the components in dialog. Contacts need to know your value and your objective.

### 5. Identify Barriers and How to Overcome Them

Using the SWOT analysis, determine your biggest barriers and design bullet-proof plans to either overcome or go around them.

### 6. Revise Your Networking List

Prioritize contacts on a spreadsheet. Set dates for contact and ongoing 4 — 6 week follow-ups.

### 7. Marshall Self-Care Resources

From professional counseling support to workout videos to scheduled "time off" activities with friends and everything else in between...get your self-care house in order.

### 8. Create a "Shoebox" Office

Your mobile office-in-a-box (or bag) should include everything from cough drops, bottled water, and tissues to a phone headset, paper, and sticky notes. Whether taking your job search into a different room or a different building, be ready.

### 9. Tie Up Loose Ends and Details

Set up your phone and computer to auto-sync. Make sure you have a professional phone message and email. Clean up your online presence. Have the car detailed and update the wardrobe. Get the small stuff out of the way.

### 10. Schedule Daily Activity Two Weeks Out

Organize your days (e.g. networking calls are best in the AM while searching online for jobs can be done at night) and fill in your calendar for at least two weeks. Specify daily goals for networking and color-prioritize various tasks. Schedule in workouts and other breaks.

# Chapter 2

## Eliminate Distractions

Set up customized systems and strategies to reduce the negative impact of the distractions in your world.

*"You can always find a distraction if you're looking for one."*
- Tom Kite

It is so difficult to get rid of distractions.

But you have to…in order to focus on job search.

No excuses.

Make it your mission to seek and destroy the distractions. For they can be your worst enemies.

Do it now…*before you get distracted*!

So, what new, simple, and easy-to-use systems can you develop that will reduce distractions and allow you to be more productive? Get creative here.

It will be important that you customize my suggestions and figure out your own solutions because your distractions may be different from someone else's.

Try out different strategies until one works. But don't give up. You have important job search tasks to perform and no time to waste.

Considering a few of the more common distractions that my clients have faced in their career transitions, I offer you the first few job search rescue strategies:

### Strategy #1

### Stop the Screen Sucking

*Reduce online distractions.* Can you hear that sucking sound? I can. It is the sound of your brain's ability to think critically and your heart's ability to care being sucked out of you into some distant void.

Don't turn into a job search zombie.

You cannot afford for that quick online search to turn into two hours of surfing.

*Put a timer with an alarm in your home office or laptop briefcase.* Next time you tell yourself that you are just going to spend 10 minutes online, set the timer and let the alarm do the rest.

But avoid using your phone as an alarm because, after all...

...you don't want to have the phone nearby as it might *add* to your distractions!

## Strategy #2
### Leave Home: Three Options

*Make a morning run to Starbucks to escape the trap of "home sweet home."* In the digital age, we hardly ever need to leave our home to conduct an effective job search. But consider the potential distractions at home: "honey do" lists on paper, other "to do" lists in your head, preparing meals, watching TV, watching the birds outside at the feeder, and munching on crap food. So, consider heading to Dunkin Donuts, Starbucks, or Panera for a coffee and some work time.

*Visit the library 2 – 3 times a week.* Any library will let you use their Wi-Fi for free, or their computers for an hour or two if you don't have a laptop. And, if the library is big enough, it will have a separate reference section with company databases and other job search resources! Whether or not you can access the library's digital databases from your home computer is irrelevant. You're trying to leave the home distractions behind, remember? Schedule in visits a couple times a week and, if you need variety, visit more than one library.

*Schedule 2 – 3 days a week at a friend's house.* Pack a lunch, laptop, smartphone, and water bottle—just like you are going to work. Which you are. You will obligate yourself to do job search. Once your friend has agreed to let you squat at their flat, *you have to do it*. And, are you going to be turning on their TV or raiding their fridge? I think not.

## Strategy #3
## Ditch the Phone

*Reduce smartphone distractions.* Your phone is a blessing and a curse. It is essential to your job search but it will do you in. Big time.

Even if you have some willpower, texting and social media temptations can just reach out of your phone, seduce you once again, and have you by the throat in no time. Five minutes of distraction here and there add up to hours each day.

There is only one solution to this problem: the trunk of your car.

Shut off the phone…and leave it in another country or at least in the trunk of your car until your resume, cover letter, emails, or other written work is complete.

And, just to be crystal clear, I did not say "leave it in another room or somewhere else in the house." *Your cell phone goes <u>in the trunk of your car</u> until your daily writing tasks are done.* Every day.

Allow yourself to check it when you take that healthy 5 minute break every 30 to 60 minutes. OK, so you might want it on "airplane" mode to boot back up quicker. But it has to be out of reach. In an inconvenient place.

Do it. Now. I'm watching you.

## Strategy #4
### Pretend You are Paying Yourself

*Commit to working smart and hard, just like you would if you were being paid.* Your next employer won't let you drift, daydream, or dawdle. So you cannot let yourself. Whether it's writing your resume, applying for jobs, or making networking calls, you need to work at it like you were being paid. Otherwise, the tasks just won't get done.

When you are unable to continue with a particular job search activity, immediately shelve that task and replace it with a different one. For example, if you are having trouble making a networking call, go work on your LinkedIn profile or send out a networking email. Just remember to eventually return to that previous task and complete it.

## Strategy #5
### Set Hourly or 15-Minute Mini-Goals

*Build momentum with short bursts of activity.* To combat distractions, set hourly, 15-minute, or even five-minute mini-goals or tasks that you will work at before engaging in any other activities.

Put the goals in your calendar and highlight them. These quick-hitter goals to complete specific tasks within very short blocks of time will boost our momentum and confidence. Once you have checked some off your list, start expanding your goals and setting aside larger blocks of time.

## Strategy #6

### Schedule Five-Minute Stretch Breaks

*Schedule five-minute stretch breaks every 30 or 60 minutes.* Not only will you be more productive over the course of a day, you will head off many potential distractions because you have already scheduled them in. That's right, think of your break as a scheduled distraction-of-sorts.

You should definitely stretch and get up to move your body for maximum physiological benefit, but you could also: play a game of two-minute online speed chess, munch a healthy snack, leaf through a magazine, check your friend's Facebook updates, or treat yourself to an actual distraction. Just make sure you limit yourself. There's always the alarm clock that you could set for a five-minute countdown...

## Strategy #7

### Take Spontaneous Breaks

*Take breaks when you need them.* Interrupt a cycle of distractions when they start, even if you have already scheduled in some breaks. And use the "five-minute rule," which I learned from a high school senior whom I was helping with college applications. It goes something like this: When you become either upset or distracted, you should not beat yourself up about it. Instead...*Accept your situation and allow yourself to be upset or distracted for five minutes. Then, move on.* Works like a charm.

### Strategy #8
### Consult a Guru

*Seek advice from a specialist.* Still having challenges in your battle with distraction or any other aspect of job search, for that matter? Then it might be time to call upon the wisdom of someone who specializes in that area.

Of course, the web is a tremendous resource, as is amazon.com. I'll admit that in my library of books I loan out to clients and use myself, there are several copies of Peter Bregman's masterpiece: *18 Minutes: Master Distraction and Get the Right Things Done*. It's on my shelf. Why not have it on yours?

# Chapter 3

## Network Smarter

Adopt new networking strategies and sincerely commit to spending 75%+ of your job search making connections.

*"The mark of a good conversationalist is not that you can talk a lot. The mark is that you can get others to talk a lot. Thus, good schmoozers are good listeners, not good talkers."*

- Guy Kawasaki

The idea of networking is often extremely distasteful and even scary. Yet the actual act of networking, once you are doing it, is often rewarding and interesting.

Obviously, you need to focus on the latter.

Because, networking should represent at least 75% of your daily job search activity if you want to gain any traction in the market, if you want to find openings that fit your background, and if you want to get noticed and interview for those openings.

Networking is the *most important* job search activity. You cannot ignore it and expect to be rescued.

<u>There are no shortcuts; you need to put in the time</u>.

This book assumes you have been networking as part of previous job search efforts and so will not get into the basics. (Note: I have included a top 10 networking tips list in the "Bonus" Chapter on page 128, if you feel you need a primer.

Instead, I will offer you a few alternative networking strategies to get you to *be more creative about the way you network*. For there is no substitute for the power of contact with other human beings!

Consider these job search rescue strategies:

## Strategy #9

### Contact Competitors Who Defeated You

*Reach out to candidates who were hired instead of you.* I'm talking about connecting with the other candidate — the one who got the job! This may be bold but it can be effective. As long as you have the right delivery. What's the angle here? Simply, the person who beat you had to come from somewhere. They were either previously employed or, just like you, they were unemployed and looking for a job.

If the person was previously employed, their old position may be open and they will have the contacts and information that could catapult you the head of the class. If the person was previously unemployed, then it's likely they have different contacts to offer and will know of other openings.

Either way, you win. If you make the call.

## Strategy #10
## Start Your Own Networking Group

*Initiate a weekly or bi-weekly networking group.* Why not? It really won't matter if five or 25 people show up to each biweekly, one- to two-hour meeting at Panera Bread or at another location of your choice.

Because the results will be both emotional and tactical support.

You'll be doing some good for others and yourself at the same time!

The format might be simple: each person is required to bring one specific request for help, such as a company or industry they want to break into.

Also, in response to another group member's request for help, each person is required to offer a contact name or some other valuable help. Of course, preferably, the group member offering help would allow their name to be used as a referral to the contact or job prospect.

You could also have the group meet in the community room of the local public library.

Especially if it has a well-stocked reference section and helpful reference librarians.

In that case, you might assign somebody new each week to bake the homemade blueberry muffins!

### Strategy #11

## Network with Past Interviewers

*Contact interviewers who didn't hire you.* By networking with people who chose not to hire you, you are showing huge confidence in your own abilities. Who knows? They might even regret not having made you an offer. Or they might be so impressed that they will think of you in a few weeks when there is another position open.

Each one of those interviewers has their own network to which they could forward your resume. Each one of these interviewers perhaps previously worked for another company to which they could refer you. And while I don't necessarily recommend that you ask for feedback, each of these interviewers could offer a few suggestions for your search. At the very least, reaching out to them will give you tremendously valuable practice at making those uncomfortable connections. Go for it!

### Strategy #12

## Reach Out to Junior-Level Contacts

*Connect with business people who have less expertise than you.* Mid- and senior- level managers may give you less time and fewer contacts because they are too busy. But junior-level persons almost never get calls from others more competent or senior to them. So, they will give you more time, more networking contacts, and more information about your target companies' cultures and potential opportunities.

## Strategy #13
## Connect Back to College

*Connect with junior-level college contacts, career advisors, and alumni at networking events.* If you attended a college, a powerful twist on the previous strategy is to network with fellow alumni from your college or university. When you contact your former school's career or alumni office and ask for a list of names to network with, you might consider targeting *alumni who graduated after you did.* You will have an instant connection with them, not only because of school, but because you will be able to regale them with stories about "the good ol' days." More importantly, you will make them feel valued by seeking their advice. They will be honored that a more senior graduate called them. And they may just very well give you the keys to the kingdom.

Also, make sure you attend any alumni events. Remember that, often times, a college or university will also have alumni clubs by state or city. FYI, if there isn't one in your town, you could always visit one nearby.

Finally, you have a unique opportunity if you can't make a scheduled event…why not be bold and reach out to the organizers and others attending? Let them know you wish you could have made it but would like to connect. Of course, you will also want to tell them that you are in the process of a career transition!

Strategy #14

## <u>Don't</u> Ask if Contacts Know of Openings

*Do not make the common mistake of asking your network contacts if they know of open positions.* Without getting into the whole psychology of a networking conversation, just think about it for a minute. Certainly, as long as you present yourself with authenticity, credibility, and graciousness, it will be a "given" that a networking contact will tell you of a position opening. As well, do not ask your contacts for advice on your resume. You will be sending your resume to each networking contact, preferably in an e-mail in advance of your conversation. So, again, of course they will make suggestions about your resume if it is warranted. <u>Your sole purpose for networking with any contact is to **get more names** for networking.</u> Anything else is a distraction for both of you and will threaten the relationship you want to build.

So, what happens if you don't ask for more names? In that case, once you have finished reaching out to the 50–100 contacts on your initial list, the well will be dry. And any accomplished sales person will tell you that *it is typically at the third or fourth level of contact referral where you will uncover the open positions for which you're well suited.*

Don't worry. People will let you know about position openings. You just need to keep adding to your network until you find the right people to connect you with the right opportunities!

## Strategy #15
## Give a Gift to a Networking Contact

*Send a modest gift to certain networking contacts.* I'm going to be honest that this is not usually my cup of tea. But, I'm including it here for a few reasons. The strategy:

- Demonstrates how bold you may need to be.
- Allows for a great deal of creativity/targeting.
- Has been successful for a few of my clients.

Use this tactic sparingly — know what to give, when to give it, and how to deliver it for maximum positive impact and no negative impact.

To be clear, I would not use this strategy as a follow-up to interviewing, only selectively in networking situations.

If a networking contact has gone "above and beyond" or is especially critical to breaking into a target company, a very modest "thank you" gift or gift card could help cement your relationship.

The best gifts are those that are useful to or valued by the receiver. It could be a new business book about a topic you two discussed. If the other person is in job search mode as well, you might even send them a copy of your favorite networking book! By the way, if you were looking for such a book, *Never Eat Alone* by Keith Ferrazzi and *Smart Networking* by Liz Lynch are both on my shelf.

## Strategy #16

## Identify 10+ New Target Companies

*Identify a new <u>rolling</u> list of target companies.* This strategy is an absolute must to include in your job-search rescue plan. Even if you have already used this strategy during a previous job search, you need to update or substantially change your list. After all, you didn't get the results you were hoping for with the old list.

Keep in mind that the term "rolling" means that companies may come and go from the list. For example, if one of the companies on your list announces a large layoff of employees, you might consider taking them off the list. Conversely, should you come across a company that has announced a hiring initiative, they could be added to your list. But these aren't just any companies.

These companies are carefully selected by you based on a fit with your background, strengths and skills, geographic preference, and a variety of other factors that are important to you.

Even if you don't end up being hired by one of these target companies, having the list will help you immeasurably when it comes to focusing your search and being proactive, rather than just being reactive and unproductively scouring the online want ads each day.

*This strategy forces you to target your networking.*

While it is certainly important to get the message about your job search out to absolutely every person you know personally and professionally, networking can easily slide into a less-productive realm in which you are just thankful for having a conversation with anyone, even the family pet!

So, when you are networking with your second cousin's uncle's brother who lives in Katmandu, your sights should still be set on acquiring names of individuals in your target companies. Or, at least with people who are in positions that are somehow connected to those companies.

As a bonus, having a list of these target companies will also force you to do company research to become familiar with industry lingo and best practices.

So, you're apt to become much more adept at business conversations as a result of focusing each day on those employers. You'll start sounding like you work there before you actually do!

And, as a second bonus, as you keep customizing your resume and conversations to appeal to this list of target companies, remember that you are actually also doing the work of becoming a more attractive candidate for positions at those companies' competitors. So, your job-search work associated with 10+ target companies is likely preparing you to apply at 40+ companies instead!

## Strategy #17

## Re-Network with Former Contacts

*Reach out to former networking contacts again.* If you have already been networking with many of these people, don't worry. You'll be connecting with them again…and again…about every 4–6 weeks.

Don't avoid calling them again because your pride or ego gets in the way – because you are embarrassed to reach out to them again – or you'll be missing out on the power of 50, 100, or however many names you had on your networking list from a previous job search.

Just as with new networking contacts, the key will be your communication beyond the initial call: in the regular follow-up over the weeks and months ahead.

Of course, you never want to "bother" a networking contact but you do want to stay "top of mind" with them. When a contact does hear about an open position or thinks of someone else for you to network with, you want the contact to think of you right away. Following up with them regularly makes a contact feel vested in your success.

Finally, please remember, whether you have spoken with them in your previous search or not, *the best contacts may be the people who are working at or connected in some other way to one or more of your 10+ target companies.*

### Strategy #18

## Make Networking Goals an Absolute

*ALWAYS meet your daily or weekly networking goal.* If you let this goal slide—even once—it's a slippery slope back to becoming a screen zombie again—applying for lots-o-jobs and getting no responses. As I've noted in several spots within the book, *you should speak with at least two new contacts each day.* Once a month or two has passed and you're also following up with a few contacts each day who you previously spoke with, the two new contacts a day will seem like plenty!

### Strategy #19

## Try These 25 Networking Quick-Hitters

*Try a couple of these simple networking tactics each week.* Because it can be challenging at first, consider these quick-hitter tactics to remind you of how easy networking can be if you make it part of daily life.

Please note that many effective ways to network are really a two-for-one special: they allow you to *give as well as get*. The key is not to try every tactic on the list but rather to <u>create your own tactics, customized around your life and your career goals</u>.

Just be ready for prime time whenever you are out in public, because there is always the potential for networking. Be mindful of your appearance and make sure your wallet contains a few business cards with your LinkedIn address on them.

Now, get up and leave the safety of the home office, show some confidence, and get networking!

To jumpstart your networking efforts, you could...

1. Train as a Red Cross CPR instructor and teach per diem or as a volunteer in area companies.
2. Attend an art gallery open house.
3. Start working out at the professionals' gym of choice during early mornings or noon time.
4. Volunteer to contact small businesses during the Chamber of Commerce's membership drive.
5. Ask friends to talk to their managers or HR to set you up with a tour of their place of business.
6. Attend a free, public event at a local university, especially if sponsored by the business school.
7. Ask a small-business person to bring you as a guest to the monthly "eggs & issues" breakfast.
8. Walk the dog in a public dog park.
9. Volunteer to join a local advisory board or community task force.
10. Identify 5 – 10 networking groups within a 25-mile radius and attend all of their meetings.
11. Go to a child's or grandchild's sporting events. Or borrow a child...root for your neighbor's!
12. Go to antique car shows. Car owners like to talk and are often accomplished professionals.
13. Start going to church again or for the first time.

14. Volunteer to solicit or give presentations at companies for the local United Way campaign.
15. Join Rotary, Kiwanis, or another service group or simply volunteer to help at their events.
16. Call your college's alumni and career offices and ask for advice networking with other alumni.
17. Attend major sporting events at your former high school or college.
18. Volunteer for a hospital's or other high profile charity's fundraising drive or events.
19. Take a job as a part-time greeter or other position at the local business school or at a business services company.
20. Offer to give a 20-minute talk with Q&A about your profession as part of an MBA career class.
21. Attend community events that are sponsored by your target companies.
22. Attend an annual dinner recognizing the area's top 10 best businesses to work for.
23. Identify the five most business-networked locals and ask them for help over coffee.
24. Join a Toastmasters club to both practice public speaking and network with others.
25. Enroll in a workshop or training that will attract employed professionals with similar skills. A few topics to get you thinking: Intermediate or advanced Excel, Supervision, Six Sigma, Customer Service, or Conflict Management. And bring those business cards with you!

# Chapter 4

## Power Up Your Resume

Revise your resume and other marketing materials to show the market your value and to interest hiring managers.

*"Never look back unless you are planning to go that way."*
- Henry David Thoreau

Revising your resume and other written material is essential to the success of your job search rescue.

Because the resume is your primary marketing tool.

This effort isn't about the past; it's about the present and future. So, you need <u>updated</u> and compelling written material. **You need to grab a reader's interest so that they want to speak with you.**

Now, as previously mentioned, this is *not* a book about job search fundamentals, such as resume writing. If you must <u>significantly</u> re-write your resume, you'll need heavy-duty assistance, such as that offered in my book, *You, On Paper: Expert Help on How to Write a Resume*.

*You, On Paper* can provide you with a more in-depth tutorial on how to (re)write your resume, should you need it. Now, let's talk resume revision!

For those of you who don't need a full re-write, the following are some strategies to consider when revising your resume or other materials:

## Strategy #20
## Add a Tagline/Brand Statement

*Add a one-line tagline/brand statement to lead your profile section.* On perhaps 20% of the resumes I write, the client telegraphs their value in a bolded, centered tagline at the top of the resume, right after the contact information and before a profile or summary paragraph. Here are a couple examples from former clients (keep in mind these will fit on one line on an 8 ½ x 11 inch page):

*Operations excellence at the intersection of ideas, people, and systems.*

**Collaborative and innovative leadership in enterprise architecture and IT strategy.**

*Guides patients to care for their own health through education, empowerment, and empathy.*

**Certified Medical Assistant and Registered Phlebotomy Technician**

Especially if you are mid- or senior-level, you could even add a tagline *after each position title,* such as:

**Founder and CEO**
*Started and grew business to $1.4M with 25+ commercial customers and 10 product lines.*

**Director, North America Human Resources**
*Controlled employment costs while maintaining positive work environment.*

### Strategy #21
## Customize with a Functional Title

*Customize for each position opening with a functional title to lead your profile section.* A few words targeted at a specific position can really get a reader's attention. Just be careful they don't pigeon-hole you for only that job. That's why I suggest using a "functional" title and not a "position" title. For example, instead of using "Manufacturing Engineer," use "Manufacturing Engineer*ing*" or, if you want to broaden a bit further, perhaps "Manufacturing and Process Engineering." Instead of "Customer Service Representative," use "Customer Service" or, perhaps, "Customer Satisfaction Focused."

### Strategy #22
## Prominently Place Hard Skills

*Highlight any hard skills that you possess and that are also critical to the position opening or market in general.* A number of candidates may say they are really adept at Excel, but how many are truly masters at pivot tables and experienced at macros? If you are, then make sure "pivot tables" and "Excel macros" are in bold and placed in the top 1/3 or "sweet spot" of the resume. Or maybe you are a welder with specialized experience in high-purity stainless welding? If you are, then make sure a reader realizes right off that you have "high-purity stainless" steel welding experience. Don't hide that light under a bushel.

## Strategy #23
## Showcase 2-3 Core Strengths

*Make sure your 2−3 top strengths are prominent.* Everyone has 15−20+ total strengths. But recruiters and hiring managers will only remember 1−3 things about you. Identify top or "core" strengths and put them front and center. An example:

> BUDGETING AND FORECASTING
> *Delivers accurate forecasts and budgets* based on customized systems that analyze organization-wide data and align with market events. Financial statement preparation and reporting integrated with up-to-date pro formas to allow for monthly review by senior management and stakeholders.
>
> CASH MANAGEMENT
> *Leads creation of detailed, automatic revenue and expense-tracking systems* as foundation to effective cash management, even in difficult situations. Maintains credit and vendor relationships during tight cash flow, while incorporating "no risk" cost reduction strategies.

Another example with slightly different formatting:

> **Avionics Technical Troubleshooting**
> Proven expertise with various guidance and control systems, including the HG 171, FulWheel Pro 2, and NNG-21. Recognized for near-perfect air readiness record. *Efficiently and completely fixes root problems.*
>
> **Teamwork and Supervision**
> Experienced in relating to diverse set of individual motivators. Known for ability to bring together heterogeneous groups and build high functioning teams. *Believes in success or failure as a team.*

## Strategy #24
## Customize Core Strengths

*Customize your core strengths for each position.* Just as everyone has many, many strengths but only 2—3 top or "core" strengths, so does a hiring manager have many, many requirements for a position but only 2—3 top requirements or hiring motives.

Once you identify these "core" hiring motives for a given position—through an analysis of the job ad, web research, and speaking to networking contacts—you need to customize the wording of your core strengths accordingly.

For example, say an open position's top-three core hiring motives are: developing pro formas, cash flow, and expense control. If the candidate in the first example of the previous strategy were to apply for that position, then they might customize their core strengths to read:

BUDGETING AND DEVELOPING PRO FORMAS
  (Optional description of core strength)

CASH MANAGEMENT AND COST CONTROL
  (Optional description of core strength)

Notice how the candidate did not entirely give up their own wording but, instead, wove in the core hiring motives.

That way they boost their **credibility** with the hiring manager while remaining **authentic** to their core strengths.

### Strategy #25
### Add Numbers

*Boost your credibility by putting numbers into your resume.* We're just going to assume that your existing resume is already chock-full of your professional accomplishments, achievements, results, etc. Because that's resume-writing 101; listing accomplishments is THE most important strategy to write an effective resume. Often, however, the strategy of including numbers gets overlooked. And it might be the second most important strategy. That's because the way the human brain works, when we read numbers (numerical values—no matter how large or small), the document's and author's credibility increases substantially. <u>Even if you only have a very few accomplishments listed because you have been in more task-oriented positions, listing numbers is a must</u>. Consider which is stronger:

Volunteered to help establish APRN pediatric clinic serving shelter families.

Or

Volunteered 10 hours/week to help establish APRN pediatric clinic serving 25+ shelter families.

**And**

Conducted early-morning patrols of housing units and adjacent wooded area every few days.

Or

Conducted early-morning patrols of 112 housing units and adjacent 450-acre wooded area 2–3 times weekly.

## Strategy #26
## Include Testimonials

*Include testimonials/quotes from your references right on the resume.* Who says that you have to save your letters of reference and/or reference list for later, in case you get interviewed? Ask permission to include an excerpt from your performance review or, perhaps, from a LinkedIn recommendation right on the resume. Just make sure to use more than one testimonial (otherwise, it appears as if only one person will vouch for you!). One way to execute this strategy is to place a testimonial after each position title but before the accomplishment bullets. So, the Navy Captain who is seeking to transition to a civilian leadership role and highlight strengths in collaboration might include a reference like this:

UNITED STATES NAVY

**Emergency Management** / *Captain – Centcom*
*"Steve's style of collaborative leadership ensures success when it comes to connecting numerous public and private entities. No one has the ability to herd cats like Steve does. Sure, he has a high level of energy, but you'll find that Steve listens acutely and never tries to force the wrong solution."* —Sid Sample, Rear Admiral

The above example is about as unreserved and straight up as they come—it will get a chuckle and get the candidate noticed. As an aside, notice how the position title has been civilianized in functional terminology…putting "Captain" first could send the wrong message to the private sector.

## Strategy #27

## Use T-Style or Bullet-Style Cover Letters

*If a cover letter is required, use a T-style or bullet-style.* Notice I said "if" a cover letter is required. As cover letters aren't widely read in today's world, don't waste your time writing one if it is not required by the hiring company (contrary to a lot of advice). If one is required, however, the most effective styles are typically T-style and bullet-style, with the web offering you numerous examples.

Combine either style with the "Customize Core Strengths" concept from a previous strategy and your cover letter might generate some interest. Identify the company's top 2–3 most important requirements. For the bullet-style, list your corresponding strengths in the middle of the letter, indented on both sides, to read something like this:

> The open position's top requirements align well with my qualifications:
>
> - 4 years of logistics coordination between 9 locations in Asia, Europe, and the Americas; 3 years inventory distribution in Hong Kong.
> - 98.7% on-time delivery in 26 months with no lost shipments.
> - BS in International Business.

The T-style is similar, with the addition of listing the company's requirements in another column.

## Strategy #28
### Use a Targeted Reference List

*Be smart about the details in constructing your reference list and include areas of strength on which your references will focus.* Your reference list can be a powerful marketing tool all by itself. Certainly, it will be customized for each position, with the 4 — 7 names chosen and ordered on the list deliberately. But, for even more value, you could add a sentence that identifies one or two (maximum) of your strengths to which the reference might speak. Then, the reference list becomes a much more versatile marketing piece, with the ability to be used alone. Consider how such a format might present the references (again, keeping in mind the width of this paper would be expanded to 8 ½ x 11 inches):

**Ida Illustration**, International Account Manager
ABC Company
000.000.0000
*Ida was a senior manager at ABC. We teamed up on a global distribution project during which Ida witnessed my conflict management and de-escalation skills.*

**Ed Example**, Logistics Director-The Americas
XYZ Company
000.000.0000
*Ed led our logistics group for 4 years and was my direct manager. He can speak to my resourcefulness and that I fit easily with all personality types.*

Just don't go overboard or you risk being perceived as "leading" instead of "informing" the reader.

## Strategy #29
### Create Addendums

*Instead of "cluttering" the resume or expanding it beyond the modern two-page limit, create additional marketing documents.* In a sense, the targeted reference list becomes an addendum. Certainly, copies of certificates or a design portfolio would be considered addendums. A recent college graduate might have a copy of a thesis or other writing samples as addendums.

Of course, you could also write up new addendum pages that would only be used to target particular application processes.

As an example, a professor or writer who is prolific in their publishing might mention only 3 – 4 of their best written works in the resume content, but then have a two-page addendum ready that lists another 15 articles. Not a writer? Well, perhaps you have received abundant training in supervision or another subject area, such that you could fill half a page with the workshops and seminars. Or, maybe it would be to your advantage to elaborate in detail on an area of expertise or particular project in a separate page, rather than lengthening your resume. Examine all aspects of your background for something that might interest the market.

Note: the font and other attributes of an addendum should match your resume, cover letter, and other documents. They are parallel in form and "look."

## Strategy #30

# Try These 15 Tips for Using the Resume

*Think both strategically and tactically when it comes to using your resume.* Don't let that fabulous re-tooled resume go to waste! Of course, you will be sending it to each and every networking contact you make and using it to apply for jobs. Consider this list of quick-hitters to boost the usability and effectiveness of your finalized resume…

1. Email your resume to yourself for availability and forwarding anywhere, anytime.

2. Attach your full resume in pdf format to your LinkedIn profile and Facebook page.

3. Create a free, professional website with Google sites and post your resume on the site.

4. Send a copy of your resume to all your LinkedIn, Google+, and Facebook contacts.

5. Drop off a physical copy of your resume at every staffing agency because they also sometimes recruit for permanent positions. Hint: be ready for an on-the-spot interview.

6. Send a copy of your resume to your college's career services office Attn: alumni career and/or employer relations staff.

7. Keep a couple printed copies in your car in a folder. Not folded or stapled together, of course.

8. Keep an electronic copy of your resume and all other materials on a CD as a full-proof backup.

9. Keep an electronic copy of your resume with you on a USB drive for access if the internet is down and you are at Aunt Mable's for the holidays. Her neighbor who works at Boeing just might want to peruse a printed copy.

8. Keep your reference list in reserve if it is not specifically asked for. Ten days after your first interview, if you still haven't heard anything, use it as an excuse for yet another follow up.

   Send it along with a 2–3-line email simply stating you are "looking forward to the next steps in the process."

9. Bring resume copies to the 2nd and 3rd round of interviews as well; don't assume the interviewers are always that organized.

10. Have 2–3 professional-looking sets of work samples or your portfolio materials to take to interviews. Don't assume you will ever get them back but don't provide crappy looking photocopies or just hand them a CD.

11. While companies still usually prefer resume submissions in Word (so they can make comments, mark it up with track changes, and so forth), provide both Word and pdf versions so at least one copy will open correctly.

    Two thoughts: Don't use just pdf as it frustrates interviewers making electronic notes on your resume before or during the interview. Also, remove all active hyperlinks (right click on your email address and choose "remove hyperlink").

12. Just as you will certainly have your phone number and email address after your name in the "signature" line of every email, add your customized LinkedIn URL or other address link where you keep a full copy of your resume attached or posted online.

13. Consider posting your resume to your profession's or industry's online job-boards that may be frequented by recruiters. Just remember to always remove or revise old resumes after your job search.

14. Visit a major library and spend some time with Kennedy Publications' *Directory of Executive Recruiters* to identify 10+ recruiters serving your industry and/or profession. In addition to recruiter referrals you get from colleagues, email your resume to each of these recruiters and follow up with a brief phone call. Just remember that, since they often make 75+ calls each day, recruiters are hard to reach and will only have a minute for you if you get through.

15. Send a copy to the appropriate hiring managers and/or HR departments at each of your 10+ target companies, even if they don't have any openings right now and even though you will still need to network into those companies. Once in a while, a resume will generate interest at the right time and the company will either create a position for you, let you know of a position expected to be open in two months, or ask you to come in for a "conversation."

## Strategy #31

## Hire a Professional

*Consider investing in professional resume-writing services if you don't think you can get your resume to A+ quality.* Don't let your ego get in the way of you presenting yourself (on paper) as the strongest possible candidate. Many of my resume writing clients have the highest level of expertise in their professions but aren't writers of marketing material. If you seek out the assistance of a resume-writer, do your research and speak with a number of prospective writers.

Most of the time, when it comes to hiring a professional resume-writer, *you get what you pay for*. $150 may be a lot of money to you. Yet, often that'll only get you a snazzy new format, a rearranging of words, and a few fancy new phrases that you might not understand. It may look great to you…and be ineffective! Depending upon your geography, your situation, and your level, it might cost $250-$350+ per page for quality, with payment up front. Also, there are no discounts for existing resumes; many of my clients have even previously paid a writer.

Even at those rates, you will still have to produce content. Many top writers assign homework. I do. Expect to have one or two conversations with the writer, in addition to providing the written content they request. Otherwise the resume will not be authentic. *You* must be in the resume.

Certifications and association memberships aren't a guarantee that a resume writer is any good, but they can be a starting point for your search. A few resume writing certifications you might be aware of include: CPRW, ACRW, and MRW. A couple of associations of which I think highly and happen to include much of the nation's resume-writing talent within their membership ranks are PARW and NRWA. Their websites will even list writers by geography.

Finally, make sure you "fit" with the resume writer. Just do not expect them to become your best friend, your career coach (unless you're paying them for that service as well), or your personal counselor. They are providing a professional service and, while you are the client, they will be in charge of your interactions. It could be a challenging collaboration if you don't connect easily with them.

# Chapter 5

## Take Action
Break out of paralysis by starting to change your thinking and using small action steps to build momentum.

*"Do you want to know who you are? Don't ask. Act! Action will delineate and define you."*

- Thomas Jefferson

"Taking action" sounds simple. But it isn't.

In fact, just thinking about the need to take action can be absolutely terrifying and paralyzing…and may result in even more procrastination or inaction! Such a quandary.

Yet, *there is no substitute for action.*

Even after you have revised your resume and have started networking, it takes effort to keep that momentum going.

So, this chapter is about how to think differently and break out of your rut of inaction, whenever it happens. This may seem scary but the truth is that while there are things you cannot control, such as the employment market, there are things you *can* control, such as taking action.

You may have been at this for over six months with no bites. You may have been working at this job search 40+ hours every week in the past with limited results. You may have witnessed your finances collapsing. You may feel exhausted and demoralized. You may have a million excuses.

But all this fear of taking action again is rooted in the past.

Now you need to *live your life in the present moment*. That's the only way you will be able to take action and then sustain your initial effort.

Because taking action in the present is the only way you're going to get out of this mess and get to the future you want and need.

You must take action.

Right now.

Now means now. Now. Today. Not tomorrow. Not on the 6th Tuesday of the month. Not after 15 more minutes with your video game, favorite TV show, or news website. All the good intentions in the world won't matter if you don't act. Now.

That's why these next job search rescue strategies involve *changing your thinking* when it comes to taking action. So, when you find it difficult to act and to get yourself to a better place, consider the following:

### Strategy #32

## Speak with Your Actions

*Action drowns out negative self-talk.* It even drowns out the negative talk of others! It certainly speaks louder than words. Let actions speak for you.

Copy down Jefferson's quote onto a sticky note and put it some place where you will see it every day, first thing in the morning. Before you hit the gym or the breakfast table, get on the computer for 10 minutes and complete just ONE action. Work on a part of your resume, send a request to network with someone you know, or research a potential job opportunity.

Then, go start your day (because you need breakfast's fuel and the workout's metabolism boost) knowing you have already taken action, already started your comeback!

### Strategy #33

## Do Your Best

*Taking action means "doing your best."* This saying is so cliché. But it's also spot on. Hey, you may have already tried your best in the past, but what about in the present? What does that look like? Be honest!

Of course, the results from doing your best can look markedly different on any given day. But <u>all any of us can ever do is our best</u>. Of course, to do your best…you must take action.

## Strategy #34

### Push Your Shoulders Back

*Action defines confidence.* And confidence is another thing you need plenty of right now. So, have one of your first actions be to change your physical stance. Just by adjusting some small details of your physicality, you will send a strong, positive message to yourself and others.

Hold that head high, push your shoulders back a bit, straighten up that arched back, and put your foot on the gas pedal. Until you feel better and more confident. And then, keep your foot on the gas pedal!

## Strategy #35

### Create Your Own Luck

*Action creates its own luck.* You cannot do anything about the market or other external factors. But you can do something about yourself. And, you know what kind of luck you are going to have if you remain in the "safety" of inaction.

So, stop complaining and start acting. Right now.

It may take hours, days, weeks, or months but if you consistently take action during every hour of every day there will be a change. If you keep focusing on taking and completing small actions during each present moment, opportunity will present itself. And, when it does…take action!

## Strategy #36

### Let Your Light Out

*Action is the arch enemy of fear and darkness.* By acting you are showing belief in yourself and letting out the light that was trapped inside you, way down deep, at your core. If you want to manage your fear, take action.

To make this strategy for changing your thinking more concrete, how about taking action to help someone else out? Even if you are so far down that you cannot take action to help yourself, you can probably take action to help out someone else. Even if it is just with a kind word or a smile. And, guess what? You just might find that such a small action to help another actually helps you out, too…you will feel better about yourself almost instantly. And in the next instant, work on that resume or reach out to a networking contact!

## Strategy #37

### Act Great

*Action defines greatness.* Have you lost sight of what your unique gift will be to the world? Well, remind yourself of it. Whether it's solving global hunger or providing the next meal for your own child. Helping the many or helping the few. Or even helping yourself, so that you're not a burden on others. None of it is possible without action. So remind yourself of the greatness within you. Then, take one step forward. Act great.

### Strategy #38

**Don't Fight Your Fears**

*Send your fears and other barriers on a vacation.* When a fear, procrastination, or some other barrier threatens to stop you from picking up the phone, dropping off a resume, or speaking up about your strengths and professional value…recognize that barrier as affecting you but also as *being separate from you*. This will allow you to start taking back control…even if it's for just a moment.

Speak to your fear or other barrier directly. Say: "Excuse me, I need to set you aside for just one or two minutes while I do this." Then, take the action you had planned: pick up the phone to make a call or speak to a networking contact. <u>Chances are, you'll be so busy taking action that you won't remember that barrier for quite some time.</u> And the next time it rears its ugly head, send it on another short vacation! *Give yourself permission to ignore that fear or barrier,* step around it, and move forward.

### Strategy #39

**Access Additional Resources**

*Research Your Situation.* If your job search is too daunting, figure out why. For example, if procrastination is a real bugger for you, pick up a copy of Jane Burka's book *Procrastination: Why You Do It, What to Do About it Now*. It's one of my go-to resources on the subject, with deep insight and good suggestions.

## Take that First Step

Hey, every one of us gets stuck from time to time.

But key to getting unstuck is both knowing that you need to assume a bit of risk and then having the courage to take that first step, to take action.

Of course, in reality you risk big things with inaction. You risk (with near certainty) that no one will know about your professional value, that you won't be considered for employment, that you won't be bringing in a paycheck, and that you won't feel good about yourself. Even if it feels safer in the moment, there is no upside to inaction.

Action, on the other hand, will:

- Move you into a different space.
- Help you get your confidence back.
- Lead to more action.

So, find your way to taking some small steps forward right now, in this present moment. Then recognize your effort and take another small step, in the next present moment. And start to build that momentum.

You can do this!

# Chapter 6

## Acquire Hard Skills

Become more marketable by making smart decisions about acquiring in-demand hard skills.

*"An investment in knowledge always pays the best interest."*

- Benjamin Franklin

Acquiring the right hard skills is one of the fastest ways to differentiate yourself in the market. *Candidates with in-demand hard skills receive more upfront interest and offers from companies.* Why?

Let's briefly review what compels any company to hire any candidate for any position. In other words, what will help them choose to hire you?

Remember, **getting hired relates directly to your ability to show hiring managers that you are the BEST CANDIDATE TO GET RESULTS—** specifically related to <u>taking away or preventing the company's pain</u> (of course, you also need to show that you will fit within their culture). It's that simple. And that difficult.

So, having *the right,* up-to-date hard skills that tie to a particular job can catapult your candidacy forward. To the interview stage. To the offer stage.

But *only* if the specific hard skills and, perhaps, any corresponding certifications, directly relate to the company's 2—3 core hiring motives. So invest the time and treasure now in securing the skills that will demonstrate your ability to get results.

What's the biggest excuse I hear for not taking action and signing up now for hard-skills training or certification classes?

"But I won't be finished with the class or program for another six weeks, three months, six months, one year, or two years…and I need a job now!"

My tough love response?

"As a non-judging observation, you have been out of work for six weeks, three months, six months, one year, or two years. If you had started such a course or program at the beginning of your job search, you wouldn't be unemployed right now. So, take a deep breath. Own your past choices. Learn from those choices. And sign up today!"

Attending skill training is also a big help in marketing yourself…in other words, when it comes to telling people about your job search. *Telling that networking contact about the course you are presently taking with your free time sounds a whole lot better than trying to defend six months of soaking up the rays on the beach or the slopes.*

Here are three strategies to consider:

### Strategy #40
## Know What Skills the Market Wants

*Do your research to identify the hard skills in demand.* Not only is it critical that you find out exactly which skills or certifications are in demand, but you also need to make sure that <u>they aren't currently in oversupply</u>!

In other words, don't just believe what you view on the web or hear from a college admissions representative. Both sources may be right about booming demand, but what about a potential oversupply? Do your research...

First, determine demand by thoroughly reviewing your target company list and the job advertisements for positions in which you're interested. You can then confirm demand and <u>inquire about potential oversupply with recent graduates and others who are presently working in the field</u>. You must employ networking and *informational interviewing* tactics with those people to verify that specific skill acquisition and/or credentialing is actually in demand, will help you *get noticed* and, potentially, *close the deal*. Then, take action.

Hint: By the way, if you are struggling to find good informational interviewing questions, the quintcareers.com site has a list of 200, easily found via a Google search.

What are some examples of in-demand skills and certifications? Here are a few to get you thinking…

- Advanced Excel, Access, and/or QuickBooks training.
- PMP certification.
- SPHR or GPHR certification.
- Welding training.
- HVAC, electrical, indoor plumbing pre-apprentice program.
- Medical assistant certification (I would highly recommend either the CMA or RMA certifications over the CCMA or NCMA ones).

## Strategy #41

### Explore Various Training Options

*Determine the best way to acquire the skills.* Don't just trust the web or some for-profit college admissions representative who is incentivized to sign you up.

Be smart about choosing your training provider.

A local adult education training may be $125 or less compared with a private provider's $300-$500 fee. And the same instructor may teach both seminars.

A local community college course may cost $300-$400 as compared with a public or private university's $1,200-$4,500 course fee. And, again, the same instructor might teach both courses!

Although companies don't usually pay for training anymore, there are exceptions. Here's one...

As you may know, welding is in demand. At an average age over 55, welders are retiring twice as fast as new hires are starting. Even in my sparsely-populated home state of Maine, there exist mobile welding training programs — some of which are free!

As an example, years ago, a company named Cianbro started providing welding courses all over the state, even in remote towns. And, if you were near the top in your class, guess who might offer you a job? That's right...Cianbro! From wire feed to arc to gas to tig to you-name-it-kind-of-welding, in certain parts of the country, welders are in demand. So, do your research and fire up that torch!

### Strategy #42
### Acquire a Certification

*Consider becoming certified as a potentially faster route to demonstrating your skills and expertise.* If you are a MCSE (Microsoft Certified Solutions Expert), you are showcasing your expertise in networking, active directory, and Windows server, among other technical areas. It's not an easy exam and usually is preceded by a study course, but such credentialing can get companies to start a conversation with you.

Do your research to identify in-demand credentialing that might be just an exam away.

# Chapter 7

## Change

Embrace the change necessary to realize different results in your new job search effort.

*"Change is the only constant in life."*
 - Heraclitus

How have things been working out? Not so well?

OK. Then it's time to embrace change. And the sooner you embrace it, the sooner you will be able to make some real progress.

Embracing change means being genuinely open to considering new approaches and assuming some risk by doing things a bit differently.

Are you are stuck in a tough, yet familiar place? Where *the known feels a lot more comfortable than the unknown*? Where it's easier to keep fiddling with a resume and applying to jobs online from the "safety" of a computer than to change your strategy? Where no one calls you because you never called them first? I know that place and I too have been there.

The prospect of change can be scary.

Because as unpleasant as that tough place is, its familiarity makes you feel safe. You're used to it. It's going to take some inertia to leave it.

But leave it you must. You must embrace the unknown. You must choose change. Even if it's dreadfully uncomfortable. Which it probably will be. But it certainly will lead to something else…

Picture yourself employed. Perhaps in a job that really fits you. In an atmosphere of mutual respect. With people you really feel comfortable around. Where you can use your skills and feel valued again. And from which a paycheck will mean you provide for yourself and, perhaps, for your family.

Maybe you don't connect with the picture I just painted? Then paint your own. But don't expect any of it to become real without change.

Why?

Do you remember Einstein's definition of stupidity? It's something like…

*Doing the same thing over and over*

*and expecting different results.*

So, here are four job search rescue strategies to help you get out of the rut of doing the same thing over and over again. Use them to make a quantum shift to develop *new* thinking and *new* actions:

### Strategy #43

### **Listen Openly to Gain New Insight**

*Listen to others without judging their words.* When you listen to others' observations or perspectives, do it with a completely open mind. You'll be surprised at the useful information you pick up about how to succeed in the market, how to get noticed by a particular company, or even how you are perceived as a candidate!

For those of us who are extroverts, that means putting aside what we are ready to say next. *Listening is not about being polite and waiting for our turn to speak; listening is about trying to understand the wisdom in someone else's words.* Start today.

### Strategy #44

### **Ask for Advice**

*Admit that you need help getting unstuck.* Start by reaching out to a few close friends or colleagues. Write an e-mail to six trusted friends and ask them for career advice. Do you have the guts to do it? Sure, you might get one crackpot response. But you just might get a gem of an idea, too.

At minimum, you'll make your friends feel valued and reengage them in your job search process. Plus, a response to your request is a person's way of saying they care about you, so you can feel valued too. And if you listen openly to what they have to say, you will probably gain useful insight.

### Strategy #45

## Do the Opposite

*Shake it up!* Try doing the opposite of what you have been doing. Or at least do something markedly different….even if that means doing the opposite of what this book tells you to do! If nothing else, it will give you a new perspective.

Here are some examples of things you could do differently: Come up with a business card that looks or feels differently from the one you have. Find a professional online discussion you can relate to via one of LinkedIn's groups, read about best practices, and post a few comments (that's called "blogging," by the way). Try dropping off a resume in person as well as submitting one via the online portal. Who knows? You may get to a different perspective…or maybe even to an interview.

### Strategy #46

## Unplug

*Define change by your non-digital actions.* While a retooled resume and LinkedIn profile may be important on your comeback tour, don't define change by what you're doing in front of the screen.

Choose to define change in terms of your non-digital actions. That includes: what comes out of your mouth, how you dress when you get up, where you go, how you deal with stress, and how many phone calls you make today.

## Strategy #47

### Simplify

*Simplify your job search and your life.* Who says that change has to be complicated? Simplicity leaves more RAM for mental computing and solving everyday problems. Simple just feels right.

Ask yourself: *"What are the one or two most important actions for job search success that I should be doing each day?"* Then, take action on those items until you get results.

You could also:

- Develop a new calendar — perhaps color-coded — that will help de-clutter and simplify your focus on the most important daily tasks.

- Brainstorm with a friend to create a list of actions you might take to make things easier and simpler.

- Take a temporary break from some ongoing personal commitments that you find draining.

- Ask friends and family members to do some of your routine tasks on a temporary basis (vacuuming and doing the dishes?) so that you have more open space and time to focus.

It's up to you *how* you embrace change. You can choose to have it feel uncomplicated and positive.

# Chapter 8

## Embrace Social Media

Know how to use social media wisely to stand out in the right ways.

*"If it scares you, it might be a good thing to try."*
- Seth Godin

Social media can make or break your job search.

It's that powerful.

Don't think that if you are over 50 that you can simply ignore it, because you will be viewed as a dinosaur and we know what happened to them. Don't think that if you are under 25 that you can simply embrace all of it without being discerning, because a negative online reputation could doom your candidacy.

Know this…

**Companies can legally require you to give them *your passwords* to Facebook or any other site if you want to be a candidate.**

I know. Tough to hear. I'm just trying to connect you to present realities. You need to get this right.

These next job search rescue strategies are focused on trying to keep you out of trouble and making sure social media becomes a positive force for you.

### Strategy #48

### Manage Your Digital Reputation

*Accurately identify and manage your digital image.* You can't address potential digital dirt if you don't know it's there. You need to check yourself out with Google, Google Alert, Yahoo, Tweet Beeps, and Socialmention.com; close accounts remotely resembling MySpace; and clean up Facebook and other social media sites you choose to leave open.

While it is difficult to remove digital dirt, if you do find any, the best strategy is to bury it by creating positive digital content about yourself. This will drive the negative stuff into a lower rank on search engines…especially if your new content is attached to an already-highly-ranked site such as LinkedIn.

### Strategy #49

### Update Your LinkedIn Profile

*Boost your digital image with your LinkedIn profile.* Make sure that your profile is fully developed (with a smiling head shot), that you belong to 10-15 groups, that you have identified 10+ "skills and expertise" for others' endorsements of you, and that you are "following" or "liking" your target companies. Also, consider attaching a full resume pdf right to your profile!

## Strategy #50
## Be Active in Three LinkedIn Groups

*Choose at least three groups in your profession or industry.* Although I would strongly recommend you do make comments on each group's blog/chat function, at a minimum you will want to read others' posts on best practices, who is hiring, and what is going on. Know that this is prime space for recruiters to frequent, so the more active you are, the more visible you are. This is social networking at its safest and, potentially, most productive.

Less interested in professional or industry groups due to geography? Do you need a "local" job? Then join more general business and industry LinkedIn groups tied to your State or geographic region. Looking for local networking events and meetings? The groups will announce them!

## Strategy #51
## Send a Consistent Message

*Integrate messaging across social media.* Sounds simple but this is often overlooked. Make sure keywords, taglines, and content are consistent on all sites: LinkedIn, Facebook, Google+, and so forth.

If your message is not consistent, recruiters and networking contacts will not understand or will be confused about your brand or professional value. Worse still, they won't know how to help you by referring you to the right open positions.

## Strategy #52

## Contact Recruiters via Groups

*Connect with recruiters via social media groups and company pages.* Millions of companies have social media pages and send recruiters online to troll for talent. So what? Five years ago, perhaps one or two of my clients were hired through a recruiter on LinkedIn. Today, ten to twenty of my clients each year are found and hired that way. You need to do all you can to *get noticed* online in the right ways.

The quickest way to attract attention, *once you have complete profiles and a consistent brand message across all your social media sites*, is to "like" your target companies and join groups. Here's a couple ways those tactics might play out for you:

- Find and be active in groups (LinkedIn), communities and circles (Google+), and communities (Facebook) connected to your background. Further *prioritize groups that include a greater number of recruiter posts*. When you see a job posted, make a comment so they know you have a similar background and ask who to contact.

- Once you have "liked" a company, look at your own news feed each day to stay current with what is going on with them. Also, research the company and then contact their recruiters with intelligent questions that show your interest.

### Strategy #53
### Add Recruiters as Connections

*Ask recruiters to be in your network.* Recruiters are usually receptive because they are building a network. Be genuine about helping them get the word out on open positions (even if those openings don't interest you) if the recruiter should ask for your assistance. Not sure if you are comfortable with this strategy? Consider this: each time a recruiter has a new position opening to fill, the *first* thing they do is let their network know about it.

### Strategy #54
### Reverse-Engineer Social Media Contacts

*Make a recruiter/hiring manager contact through a reverse engineering strategy.* If you see a job posted by a recruiter or hiring manager on Indeed.com, Simplyhired.com, Monster.com or another job board, simply go to LinkedIn and other social media sites and contact the recruiter or hiring manager that way. You have a much greater chance of standing out.

### Strategy #55
### Find Recruiters via Your Contacts

*Peruse your LinkedIn contacts to find recruiters with whom they are linked.* Then, politely ask each contact for recruiter referrals. Be gracious enough to do the same for them. You could even offer the names of a couple recruiters when making your request.

## Strategy #56
## Leverage Facebook

*Use Facebook in your job search.* The challenge with Facebook is that it is predominantly about the personal side of your life, while LinkedIn is focused more on the professional side.

However, there are a number of ways you should consider leveraging Facebook.

Here are three tools that help make Facebook more useful for your job search:

- **BranchOut** is a database for professional profiles where thousands of recruiters search. It may connect you to some interesting opportunities. BranchOut is also effective in messaging with co-workers. Unfortunately, its future as a job search tool has become less clear and, in 2014, its assets and tech team were acquired. So, use it now!

- **InTheDoor** shows you companies that are hiring and is one way to determine the companies where your contacts are employed.

- **Graph Search** is a tool that Facebook suggests will help you make "connections between people, places, and things." You can type in the name of a product, company, or job you are interested in and then search contacts for anyone who is using that particular word or phrase.

## Strategy #57
## Tweet Your Way to a Job

*Consider integrating Twitter into your search.* Like Facebook, Twitter is not set up to easily serve your professional or job search needs. The power of Twitter, however, is growing fast. Here are a few thoughts if you choose to tweet during your search:

- Your **Profile** should be professional with your name integrated into your "handle" and a headshot with smile (you might use the same one on all the social media sites with which you are involved). Your **Bio** should be succinct and have a professional title and keywords that show your value and skills.

- **Hashtags (#)** can help you search for relevant information on the Twitter site (e.g. #engineerjobs lets you see tweets about engineering jobs that others have tagged). Hashtags show perhaps Twitter's biggest advantage for job search purposes…<u>your use should be less about broadcasting and more about *listening* to what is going on.</u> This includes identifying recruiters and hiring managers, as well as networking contacts and opportunities at your target companies.

- Follow companies and "like" recruiter posts to help you get noticed in the right ways. Even if you find something that is not your personal cup of tea, you can still re-tweet it for the benefit of others.

# Chapter 9

## Write

Use your writing skills to *get noticed* by key networking contacts and hiring managers.

*"A writer who waits for ideal conditions under which to work will die without putting a word on paper."*

- E. B. White

The written word is powerful; powerful enough to get you noticed.

Sure, there are a lot of people blogging, tweeting, posting…tapping their keyboard into oblivion. But most of them are doing so for their own fulfillment and often share random or personal information that is not of interest to hiring managers.

Of course, there's nothing wrong with writing for personal reasons. But imagine the power of writing just a few pieces — perhaps about industry or professional best practices — and sharing them with networking contacts or folks working at your target companies.

Difficult? Maybe.

Game changing? Absolutely.

You don't have to be a master at words or be an expert in a particular area to pen something interesting, powerful, and useful. Something that reflects well on you and your initiative, your research ability, and your courageousness in putting your ideas out there.

This could set your candidacy apart, big time.

Here are a few job-search rescue strategies:

### Strategy #58
### Blog

*Create your own blog or join in on another's.* You don't have to create your own blog, you can start posting your thoughtful comments on professional and industry website blogs that are frequented by others with similar professional backgrounds.

LinkedIn groups are good places to start, as they are frequented by recruiters and typically offer higher-quality discussions. You are supposed to be joining a number of LinkedIn groups anyway, so simply pick 2–4 groups to follow and join in!

To get over your writer's block, read a couple web articles on the elements of effective blogging. And hit the keyboard hard. Even if you don't get an interview directly from the blogging, think of the talking points you will have during your next networking or interviewing conversation…from your own writing and from reading others' posts.

## Strategy #59

## Develop White Papers

*Write up 3 – 6 white papers of 2 – 4 pages each.* Wait a minute. What is a white paper, anyway?

Well, it's like a blog post but a bit longer and usually more well-researched. And, just like a blog post, it doesn't have to be full of your original ideas. Rather, it could examine best practices and present them in a manner that is useful to a professional or industry community.

How do you get going on such a project? Reading high-quality blogs about best practice ideas by subject-matter experts is a good start. Of course, you will be absolutely sure to cite those experts, giving them credit for their ideas when you write your white papers. Get over that thought that your writing has no value unless you create original concepts. Both blogging and writing white papers are less about how original or creative you are and more about sharing, showing professional kindness, and making a difference in the lives of your peers. Get it? This is less about the writer (you) and more about the reader (them).

In fact, you will come across as more humble, knowledgeable, resourceful, and connected to best practices by citing others. When a hiring manager reads your work, they will think of you as a team player who recognizes the contributions of others.

Imagine the impact that these white papers will have when you present them in an interview. They instantly become "addendums" to your resume; they are part of your portfolio.

They will set you apart from the competition.

So that you can *close the deal*.

### Strategy #60

## Post Links to Articles on LinkedIn

*Post helpful links to your LinkedIn "share an update" newsfeed.* Can't think of anything to write? No worries. After reading my advice about writing white papers, I hope you now realize that <u>helping others by sharing quality content is the key</u>.

The whole objective here is not to produce something original (remember how you need to ditch your pride but boost your confidence?).

The objective is to be helpful to others and, as a result, perhaps get noticed.

A win-win.

Pick a reputable source for print or video, maybe either the Wall Street Journal's online edition or something from TED.com. Write a few lines summarizing the link's content and send it out. Of course you could always rise to the occasion, write a blog post, and send that link out as well!

## Strategy #61
## Send Writings to the Hiring Manager

*Send a copy of your blog article or white paper directly to the hiring manager.* Why keep your writing a secret from the very people who control interviews? That top-quality article or blog post on industry best practices you just wrote or co-wrote should go directly to the hiring managers at your target companies, as well.

Learning from the strategy above about posting links on LinkedIn, *if you can't bring yourself to write much more than a few lines in summary of someone else's article or help-video, you could still send that along with the link to their work.* As long as it is top quality and relates both to the hiring manager and your candidacy. It must create a link between you two.

What do I mean by relating to both of you? Well, imagine that you have researched a target company and they are in the middle of a big conversion: introducing XYZ software to improve inside sales. Perhaps you have inside-sales experience and were part of a conversion — even if it was a different software package — years ago, but you can't get your resume past HR. Find an article that gives helpful hints about conversions with XYZ software, write a brief summary, and email the article and summary to the hiring manager directly. You could even include your resume. What have you got to lose?

## Strategy #62

### Interview the Hiring Manager

*Interview potential hiring managers as part of your blog article or white paper.* Who says that hiring managers are the only ones who do the interviewing? If you are feeling really bold, why not pick a topic of interest to a group of hiring managers and then interview several for your article? I know of several people who market themselves very effectively using this technique.

Not feeling quite that bold but like the idea of relating a topic directly to an individual hiring manager?

Search the web for any derivations of the hiring manager's (or their boss') name combined with their current or past company/employer's names. Or, identify which LinkedIn or other professional groups they belong to, read blog posts they may have made, and note which companies, organizations, or thought leaders they may be "following" on LinkedIn. You could also network with people who know the hiring manager.

When you determine what will peak their interest, research the subject matter and write a white paper or blog about it. Then, let them know about your writing. Additionally, you could even ask for their opinion on your words.

You will have their attention.

## Strategy #63
## Write a Market Review of a Company

*Research and write a company or product review.* You should be involved in extensive market research involving your target companies anyway. So why not go even further and create a one- to three-page executive summary of your findings and send them along to the hiring managers at those companies?

The focus of your research could be: market analysis of their service or product, brand reputation and/or recognition, positioning against their competition, or market potential for new offerings. Include a graph or other data to make it standout. Some of my clients had even visited multiple retail locations as a "secret shopper" (this is easy with banks and other retail or service organizations) so they could comment on a firsthand experience.

Does this bold approach involve a lot of sweat equity and carry a slight risk of putting off the representatives of the hiring company who may not agree with your report's conclusions? Sure, there's an outside chance. But there is even more of a chance that you will get noticed, have the opportunity for some dialogue, and be recognized for your initiative.

Hey, we are working with the premise that your job search is stalled at the moment. Why not jump start it and get back on the road?

## Strategy #64

## Create a 30—60—90 Plan

*Develop a plan of what you would do during your first 90 days on the job.* This strategy is especially effective and routinely used by new college graduates. While it carries some risk for job seekers in the middle to later parts of their careers, it may still be an acceptable risk for you to take, considering the tremendous potential upside.

For years, companies have asked candidates — especially recent college graduates — to develop a 30 — 60 — 90 plan as part of the interview process.

But you can take the initiative and send one to the hiring manager to get noticed and increase your chances for an interview.

As with the "Market Review" strategy, there is risk related you making incorrect assumptions.

But if you can produce a high quality product, the hiring manager will usually overlook some incorrect information because they're so <u>impressed with your initiative</u>.

Finally, why not consider utilizing this strategy with several competitor companies simultaneously? You are already doing the research. Just customize the 30-60-90 plan for each company. I bet at least half your research and writing time will be relevant in marketing yourself to multiple organizations.

## Strategy #65
## Write a Letter to the CEO

*Write a letter telling the CEO that you are interested in working for their company and follow up with a phone call.* Talk about a bold approach. But, why not? This strategy was traditionally a staple of the middle- and senior- manager's job search, back in the day.

Take special care with its implementation. Sending paper (which can sometimes get you past the administrative gate keeper) has the potential of labeling you as out-of-date in our digital world. And sending directly to the CEO by any means risks you being perceived as trying to bypass HR and hiring managers. But some of my clients have pulled this off and even generated interviews.

Often, the CEO or assistant will send your letter and resume to HR or a hiring manager. But that means it gets to a real person…and via the CEO!

Targeting a minimum of 25 companies to approach in this labor-intensive effort is critical to generate even the smallest results. As long as they made follow-up phone calls, my clients have often had a response rate of 5−10%. That response rate is a whole lot better than what you'll get by submitting your resume online/through an applicant tracking system.

Just make sure you execute this tactic flawlessly.

# Chapter 10

## Boost Confidence
Feel and show more confidence by reminding yourself of your professional value.

*"Nobody can make you feel inferior without your consent."*
- Eleanor Roosevelt

Get rid of pride. But boost your confidence.

Pride often works against you. Confidence works for you. How so?

Pride is ego-based and seeks to serve itself. *It can quickly turn into self-congratulation*. It will not let you ask for help when you need it the most. It cringes when it thinks of you reaching out to certain people for help in times of need. It won't let you apply for a position that it determines is "beneath" you.

Confidence seeks to serve you. It is based on accessing the thoughts and feelings that reside deep inside of you. *Confidence is about <u>remembering</u> that you trust yourself*. Remembering that you are professionally competent, remembering that you really care about doing a good job, and remembering that you treat others with dignity, respect, and kindness.

Confidence is really always right there beneath the surface. It's just natural to forget about it sometimes. So, now it's just time to remember by letting these job search rescue strategies guide you:

### Strategy #66
## Schedule Quick Confidence Boosters

*Schedule in a quick confidence booster every day.* To remind yourself that you are confident, open up your calendar and schedule in a confidence booster each day. Otherwise, you'll forget or put it off. Forever. And you're going to need regular confidence boosters to ride the emotional roller coaster of your job search and keep motivating yourself to take action. You can come up with your own, but here are four confidence boosters to get you started:

- Examine the results and skills on your revamped resume.
- Read the praise on past performance reviews.
- Brainstorm a list of all your strengths, values, and positive personality traits.
- Find and listen to high-quality, high-impact motivational videos or read blog posts to get other ideas on how to boost your confidence. Watch Harvard Business School Professor Amy Cuddy's TED.com presentation on how body language and power posing can really boost your confidence.

### Strategy #67

## Turn Weaknesses into Strengths

*Look at yourself as a "whole person."* We each have weaknesses. But, inherent in nearly every weakness is also a strength. Examples? Impatience can often translate into efficiency. Being social can suggest an ability to fit in with a broad range of personality types. And being obstinate can mean you have strong beliefs or values.

Make a list of all your weaknesses. Then, remind yourself that inherent in every weakness is a strength. Identify those strengths and write them down on a separate piece of paper. File the weaknesses paper in the circular file. Affix the strengths paper to your fridge or place it on the wall near your computer. Read it every day.

### Strategy #68

## Ask Others to Boost Your Spirits

*Delegate confidence-boosting to others.* External validation is an important part of reminding us of our professional value and self-worth. When a professional colleague next asks you what they can do to help with your job search, ask them if they would be amenable to giving you a 10-minute pep talk once a week, during which they will remind you of your professional strengths and accomplishments. Then, schedule it into your calendar for the next eight weeks.

### Strategy #69

## Use Your Professional Strengths

*Keep using your professional strengths and skills.* Avoid one of the hidden traps of any prolonged job search: Not feeling valued anymore because you aren't using your work-related skills and abilities. Whether you are paid for your effort or not, there is tremendous upside to investing some time each week to use your professional strengths. Why not consider:

*Volunteer as an Individual Contributor*
Volunteer a few hours a week in an adult activity that is directly related to one of your core strengths.

If you are an accountant, volunteer to help balance the books at your local church. If you are a salesperson, volunteer to help fundraise for your favorite charity. If you are an auto mechanic, volunteer to help fix the buses at a community transportation organization.

You will get paid in good feelings and reminders of your professional value. You will also have another item to go on your resume.

*Volunteer as a Mentor or Teacher*
Volunteer, formally or informally, to help teach or mentor another adult or a child in your area of expertise. It could be in a formal classroom, adult education evening seminar, or in your backyard.

If you are an accountant, teach a junior achievement class or provide free tutoring for accounting students at your local high school or community college. If you are a salesperson, volunteer to help the local youth group or one of its individual members with an upcoming fundraiser. If you are an auto mechanic, volunteer to help out at your local vocational school's automotive technology class or teach your son or daughter how to change their own brake pads (or at least their oil).

If you choose to teach and mentor adults, you might even find that some of them are working in companies on your target list. Instant networking!

# Chapter 11

## Take a Team Approach
Leverage the concept of *team* throughout your job search.

*"In union there is strength."*
- Aesop

Asking for—and accepting—the help of others is just plain difficult for most of us. Indeed, it's one reason networking is so distasteful to many. We are hard-wired to mind our own business and make our own way. When it comes to job searching, however, you need to swallow your inner maverick and adopt team strategies.

Because if you don't, it's going to be a lot harder—if not impossible—to successfully job search.

You *need* to involve others in your search.

Opening up to the idea of team means opening up to constructive criticism, new ways of doing things, potential new directions, and leaning on others.

That could be a lot of change for you. If you happened to skip over the chapter on change, this might be a good time to go back and take a look!

You are probably familiar with the concept that TEAM can stand for *Together Everyone Achieves More*. Embrace that thought. So, even though you are leading this job search rescue mission, you don't go at it alone!

Following are a few job search rescue strategies related to the concept of team:

### Strategy #70
### Recruit a Job Search Team

*Approach 5 – 10 individuals about helping you with your search.* These may include family, friends, peers, subordinates, supervisors, or people acting as your references.

They don't need to ever get together as a group but they will commit to allowing you access to their knowledge, resources, and time, whether it be for networking strategy, market and target company information, their networking contacts, access to social or business events, or emotional support.

### Strategy #71
### Assemble a Resume Review Team

*Ask 4 – 6 individuals to give you feedback on your resume and all written materials.* Even if you have your resume professionally written, you'll want to find recruiters, hiring managers, and others to critique it. Ask for their objective view in examining both detail and big picture perspectives.

## Strategy #72
### Team Up with Salespersons

*Add salespersons to your team.* Salespeople have the ongoing job of getting noticed by their prospects and client companies, as well as closing the deal on new business. Why not seek out a couple of them as volunteer-advisers to your job search effort? If they've been in sales for a while, they are probably getting results. Let them help you come up with creative ideas for networking and marketing yourself, as well as the most effective ways to both execute those ideas and negotiate an offer.

## Strategy #73
### Organize a Resume Blitz

*Organize a family and friends resume blitz.* Contact 15–20 family members and friends. Ask each person to send out your resume to at least 10+ of their best contacts. Write a brief but compelling letter of introduction and make it the first page of your electronic resume attachment so that it is actually part of the resume itself and is viewed first.

Ask your family and friends to complete this favor by the end of the week and, when it is done, to send you a quick e-mail letting you know. That will help keep them on task and honest, as well as minimize the need for any follow up on your part. Except, of course, some personal, hand-written thank you letters and other expressions of appreciation to your team members.

## Strategy #74

### Recruit a Truth Team for Big Changes

*Approach 3–6 people to serve as an objective "truth team" if you are planning big career changes.* Just like your job search team, these folks never need to get together in a group; you might request their individual thoughts on a monthly or bi-monthly basis. Their value will be more strategic and less about detailed tactics. A couple members of this team should know the business landscape very well so that they can counsel you on market challenges.

If you are planning to make a big career shift—including the idea of catapulting yourself from a senior managerial to executive level, for instance—you could recruit a separate truth team that is even more strategic in nature. Keith Ferrazzi expertly expands on a similar concept in his book *Whose Got Your Back*. It's on my shelf, along with his *Never Eat Alone* book. If you are looking to climb the ladder big time, you'll want to avail yourself of his work.

## Strategy #75

### Recruit an Accountability Buddy

*Partner with someone to help keep you accountable.* Having at least one "accountability buddy" is mandatory for you. Because you are your own worst enemy. You can't trust yourself to do work you don't want to do. (Neither can I, by the way.) That is why I often use the accountability buddy concept to help me do the things I don't want to do.

There are many variations to the concept but it essentially works like this: On Monday morning you and your accountability buddy will e-mail each other with a short, manageable task list that you have devised for the week. The list represents the <u>most hated tasks</u> that you need to accomplish. Perhaps it is: networking with two new contacts each day, or reaching out to a family member for help, or applying for three positions that require swallowing your pride. You decide. But it must be *hated, loathed, reviled, despicable, detested, abhorrent* tasks...that need to get done.

On the honor system, at the end of the week, you report back to your buddy on your progress. If you have not done 100% of your list, you pay a pre-arranged, *hated, loathed, reviled, despicable, detested, and abhorrent* penalty. Like sending a $100.00 check to a political candidate or charity *that you <u>don't</u> believe in*. I don't know what your penalty should be. Just make sure you really, really, *really* hate it.

Statistically, you will probably have to pay the penalty once, sometime around week three or four. But, after that, you will be right as rain for the rest of the journey. Can you handle it? <u>This is a strategy that could make or break your job search rescue by keeping you honest, motivated, and on task.</u> Now go find your accountability buddy!

# Chapter 12

## Talk the Talk
Learn to speak confidently and professionally when networking and in the interview.

*"The single biggest problem in communication is the illusion that it has taken place."*

- George Bernard Shaw

You need a public speaking boot camp.

Why? Well, because the silver-tongued, pandering candidates don't get hired. The articulate, confident candidates do.

Know that form can be as important as content here. The messages taken away from spoken communications are 90%+ nonverbal. Of course, the content of your words better be of substance and be compelling. But your delivery must help your message be clearly understood and prioritized by the listener.

Facial expressions, tone of voice, body posture, the use of hands, and other factors contribute to whether you will be just politely acknowledged or really heard. <u>If you need to reboot your job search, you need to reboot your public speaking as well.</u>

So how can you up your game in this area? Here are five job search rescue strategies that have worked in the past for my clients:

### Strategy #76
## Record Yourself

*Review an audio or audio-visual recording of yourself.* This recording would be of your 30–60 second answers to standard interview or networking questions. In this digital age, this is easily accomplished via laptop web cam or smart phone.

Make the experience more real by asking a trusted friend or family member to ask the questions. Add more depth to the analysis by selectively sharing the recording with the trusted advisors on your job search team. Just don't post it on the web.

### Strategy #77
## Attend Group Meetings

*Join a church or civic group and participate in meetings.* This is one of the easiest ways to become more comfortable in a group situation and it affords numerous opportunities to practice your public speaking and social protocols.

Dress business casual for every meeting, go prepared, speak up, volunteer to present on topics, and improve your listening skills, as well as your confidence at public speaking. It also offers you the chance to make more networking contacts!

### Strategy #78
### Read a "How to" Book

*Access web or print advice on networking, fundraising, or selling.* One of my personal favorites is Dale Carnegie's *How to Win Friends and Influence People*. Another oldie but a goodie. <u>Just remember to practice what you have learned.</u>

### Strategy #79
### Volunteer in a Sales Role

*Volunteer in a sales or fundraising role.* Sign up with United Way, the American Red Cross, or another worthy organization to solicit donations or recruit volunteers. You'll be helping others at the same time as you'll be helping yourself. If the organization's training for your new role is not up to par, make it your mission to seek out best practices in fund raising and solicitation via the web and then put them into action.

### Strategy #80
### Join a Toastmasters Group

*Locate and join a Toastmasters club.* With over 250,000 members in 12,000+ clubs worldwide, they have to be doing something right. Meetings of 15–20 people for one to two hours each are typical. And they will force you to improve both your delivery and your confidence in speaking publicly. Sounds good but just too scared to take action? Call a buddy and do it together. You will love the result!

# Chapter 13

# Go Where You're Trusted
Make the job search easier by connecting with people who already trust your value as a professional.

*"Trust is the glue of life. It's the most essential ingredient in effective communication. It's the foundational principle that holds all relationships."*

- Stephen Covey

Any port in a storm.

Statistically, there are three best strategies for getting hired when you are really down and out or the economy has its foot on your throat. These strategies are:

- Contacting former employers.
- Contacting competitors of former employers.
- Contacting former co-workers.

The reason these strategies are so effective? *Trust.*

All three groups trust your professional value. You have a track record with former employers, even if it was five years ago. The competitors of former employers will instantly appreciate your value and speak your language. Former co-workers have actually seen you in action.

OK, so there might be one or two companies or persons whom you really don't want to work for or who don't want to hear from you. Cross those off the list and get down to business.

Here's a job search rescue strategy for each:

### Strategy #81
## Contact Former Employers

*Reach out to former employers to get hired or referred.* Former employers are low hanging fruit because:

    a. They know your value; you are low-risk.

    b. You already know people who are or were at those companies so you know you would fit with them.

Think about it. Companies today hire people who say they want to work and then, when the new people aren't promoted to supervisor or get a raise within a couple months, companies' attrition rates skyrocket. Sure, companies prize the stamina of youth but they also covet good decision-making and commitment. Even if they don't have a position for you right now, there's always next month.

### Strategy #82
## Contact Competitor Companies

*Reach out to competitors of your former employers to get hired or referred.* Guess where a bunch of your former co-workers ended up? At competitors.

And guess how your former co-workers were hired at competitors? They were referred or vouched-for by other former co-workers who had made the transition before. This could be your ticket in, too.

So what if your skills are a bit rusty and you've been out of the industry for a few years? Certainly, before making contact, you'll want to research the latest best practices and you might even find a seminar to brush up on your Excel or welding skills, if those are in demand at that company. Leave your pride at home and show your confidence that you could add value with less training time than most hires.

## Strategy #83

### Contact Former Co-workers

*Find and network with former co-workers.* Former co-workers can often be found on Facebook, LinkedIn, or through mutual connections—people who used to work with both you and them.

Regardless of where your former peers are now employed, they will likely take your call and understand your value. It's very possible that these former coworkers are now working in a very different kind of position at a company that is unlike the one at which you both worked all those years ago. So what? That just demonstrates their ability to relate to your situation. And your need for something new. For a fresh start. It might be at their company or another one they know about.

# Chapter 14

## Make Better Decisions
Put strategies in place to help you realize improved results from your choices throughout the job search.

*"It is your decisions, and not your conditions, that determine your destiny."*

- Anthony Robbins

Tony Robbins is so right.

Since this is a job-search rescue, a number of you reading this may not be in the best of conditions — financially, emotionally, psychologically or even physically. And, while you can't change the environment around you overnight, you do hold the ultimate power of choice in how you think, feel, and act.

So, this chapter will give you a few new strategies to try in your effort to make better decisions.

Because, without better decisions, the odds are that you will eventually wind up right back where you started. And I don't want that for you. I want you to have more choices, better conditions, and a brighter future.

Obviously, if you are considering new concepts around decision-making, you might benefit from a review of the chapter on being open to and embracing change. After all, our decision-making bias is reinforced every day with the hundreds of small decisions we make. So you are going to need to dig deep for the courage to try some alternatives and to create new decision-making models that work for you in certain situations. After all, you are a unique person and you will require a unique solution to make better decisions.

And, as usual, there is no short cut. You have to do the heavy lifting.

So get online and further explore the following strategies, modifying and trying them until you are making better decisions:

### Strategy #84
## Decide to Decide

*Commit to decision, not indecision.* In the moment, it is so much easier and less painful to put off decision-making. But that will get you nowhere fast.

Remember the chapter on action vs. inaction? Well, that's what I'm talking about here, as well. We all have built-in tendencies to procrastinate around making certain decisions. So, you need to recognize those tendencies in yourself and fight against them.

More time doesn't always mean a better decision.

## Strategy #85
### Be Bold; Lead Yourself

*Be bold in your decision-making in order to lead yourself into the future.* True leadership means making decisions based on imperfect or limited information, such as that found earlier in a decision-making cycle. Years ago, Christensen and Kreiner discovered that successful leaders understand this and tend to *make bolder decisions sooner* so that their decisions will have greater impact. The longer you wait, the more information you will have but the less impactful your decisions will be. True, a few of the decisions made earlier will be wrong, but the much greater impact of right decisions will more than outweigh the few wrong ones. Collect some information and then…be bold.

## Strategy #86
### Resolve Conflict by the Situation

*Develop a situational approach to making decisions around conflict.* Most conflict involves people and tasks. Therefore, decisions about how to behave or what to say in conflict can be among the most important to get right. Use a system to analyze the conflict situation and de-personalize it to make better decisions. In trainings, I often suggest people consider leveraging the TKI's (Thomas-Kilmann Conflict Mode Instrument) five modes: compete, collaborate, compromise, accommodate, and avoid.

It could help you reduce *potential* conflicts, too.

## Strategy #87

### Use Decision-Making by Quadrant

*Adopt easy-to-remember quadrant-models of decision-making.* There are many four-quadrant models of decision-making. Since you can picture them in your mind, they are often easier to recall and, therefore, more often utilized than other models. Here are three of my favorites to explore:

**Johari Window**: Helps you understand how your personality interacts with the external world and with the quadrants: what you know about yourself but others don't know, what you know about yourself and others know as well, what you don't know about yourself but others happen to know about you, and what you don't know about yourself and others also don't know.

**DISC**: Following Jungian thinking, Marston's DISC looks at personality-related behavior—suggesting you might choose different behaviors to maximize your effectiveness in human interactions, depending on another's behavior. The four quadrants are sometimes referred to as: Drive, Influence, Steady, and Compliance.

**Eisenhower Model**: Developed by the Supreme Allied Commander and efficiency expert himself, these quadrants help with deciding when tasks should be accomplished and are influenced by "important" v. "urgent" axis: do it now, schedule it to do later, put it off, and delegate it out.

## Strategy #88

### Consider Intent v. Impact

*If you can remember that <u>each person's perception is their reality</u> you will markedly improve your interactions with others.* Certainly, you should always be authentic or true to yourself. However, you should also be thinking about how your words and actions impact others. Especially considering the context of a job search, in which you need to boost credibility with others to get noticed and close the deal. Good intentions are important. But allowing yourself a quick check-in during the moments before you open your mouth or hit "send" on an email can be the difference between speaking "at" someone or really connecting "with" them.

## Strategy #89

### Think AND Feel

*Find the right balance between objectivity and subjectivity.* Since when did feelings become a bad thing in decision-making? For some people, their "gut" feeling is one of the keys to making good choices. Important here is knowing the right balance for yourself in certain situations.

You probably don't need to take a Myers-Briggs assessment to find out if your decision-making is influenced more by feeling or thinking. But keeping the awareness of your preferences in your conscious mind can certainly help you make better decisions for the person who you really are.

## Strategy #90

### Use Pull-Pull Instead of Balance Sheet

*Improve your objective decision-making by comparing apples to apples.* Whether it is deciding on applying for a position, what strategy to use in an interview, or if you should take a job offer, the balance sheet or "+/-" approach is a common method of objective analysis that compares the "pros" with the "cons." Unfortunately, we easily forget that "pros" and "cons" are like apples and oranges; they are different. It can be more useful to objectively examine what is "pulling" you in one direction (say, toward accepting an offer) and what is "pulling" you in the other direction (toward declining the offer). Make two lists side-by-side and compare them for a more objective insight. Be authentic or true to yourself, however.

## Strategy #91

### Talk with Others to Gain Clarity

*Talking it over with others can help with clarity, <u>as long as they are not influencing you</u>*. You must make your own decisions but, sometimes, trusted advisors can provide new observations and insights. Also, remember that, if you are an extrovert, you will not be able to process and analyze to your maximum potential <u>unless you actually hear yourself speak out loud</u> (for example, you need to speak the factors that are "pulling" you in each direction). Just find a patient person to sit there and listen to you!

## Strategy #92
### Separate Needs from Wants

*Be clear about your needs and wants and <u>meet your needs first</u>.* Basing decisions on your wants is perfectly legitimate…as long as you are already meeting your needs! Otherwise, you will be kicking yourself in hindsight. It's an age-old problem, of course. Consider any number of little, everyday decisions and how much our materialistic culture influences us to have our wants met immediately. Use a humanist model such as Maslow's to define needs (physiological, safety and security, love and belonging, esteem, and self-actualization) to keep yourself honest.

## Strategy #93
### Know When to Call in the Cavalry

*Don't wait until it's too late; you can't make good decisions if your thinking is off.* I am not advocating that you get out your checkbook right now. I am saying that it is human nature to incorrectly think we can dig ourselves out of a deep hole. <u>Even if you *think* you are making good decisions, listen to the input of those around you; if everyone is saying otherwise, consider getting help.</u> Whether it is an assist from a resume writer, career coach, personal counselor, or dress-for-success consultant that you might need…do your research, interview them, and get the right fit earlier rather than later. And, remember, you usually get what you pay for.

# Chapter 15

# Re-Introduce Yourself

Be deliberate about how you reintroduce yourself and your brand to the employment marketplace.

*"You never get a second chance to make a first impression."*
   - Oscar Wilde

Yet, in this case of rebooting your job search, you are, indeed, giving yourself a second chance. So, the quote's context should really relate to first impressions *this* time around. Bottom line: don't blow it.

Did you know that you have two seconds to make a first impression?

That's according to the well-written author, Malcom Gladwell, in his book *Blink: The Power of Thinking Without Thinking*. And I would agree.

So, you have to attend both to the macro and the micro here. No detail should be overlooked. And, remember, <u>there are no shortcuts</u>. Not if you want results this time around. And, for those of you who have just conducted a job search sometime in the past year, you are really going to be under a microscope.

Don't overlook the importance of that re-tooled resume or presenting yourself confidently, but also don't overlook these job-search rescue strategies for making a positive first impression:

## Strategy #94

### Don't Be Defensive

*Never come across as defensive.* After all, a job search is about playing offense, not defense. If you come across as defensive, people will view you as negative and not in the frame of mind to be a strong candidate.

Be honest, matter-of-fact, or even bold, but never be defensive. For example, if you have chosen to take time off to deal with a family situation (perhaps both you and the company didn't want it to impact your work), just put it out there. What is the matter with that? Family always comes first.

## Strategy #95

### Don't Show Shame or Guilt

*Showing shame or guilt will mark you as damaged goods.* Even though there is a huge difference between shame and guilt, you can't show either. It will quickly taint your image and you will not be hired. Or even interviewed. Hey, the past is the past. So, own up to it and move on.

Besides, almost everybody loves a good comeback story. So, give it to them!

## Strategy #96

### Be the Comeback Kid

*Act like you are in-demand and you will be.* Never come across as arrogant, but make sure people notice you are confident in your abilities and skills. This will require you to be sensitive to both your delivery and the content of your words—don't assume folks remember the value you offer. And don't hide from previous job search or job failure. That would only be inauthentic. After all, this is a *comeback* so it is perfectly OK to admit your tactical mistakes (like dying your hair green for that final round interview?). Let the world know that you have learned and that you are back!

## Strategy #97

### Don't Apologize

*Whether the failure of your last job search was your fault or not, never apologize.* This one could be particularly tough for you but, please understand…an apology is essentially an admission of guilt! Even if you made mistakes, your networking contacts, recruiters, and potential hiring managers are not people to whom you should be apologizing.

Especially if you are out of work through no fault of your own (a reduction in force or layoff at a company, for instance), do not do anything other than hold your head high. You may feel like you want to apologize, but do not.

## Strategy #98

## Show What You Have Been Doing

*Let people know how you have <u>invested</u> your time, especially if you were not working at all.* Notice I said how you have "invested" your time and I didn't say how you have "spent" your time. A subtle, yet important, difference.

Preferably, of course, you have something of professional value to show for your time out of work. If not, then you need to *immediately* run — not walk — and secure a couple meaningful and value-adding activities. These might include: volunteering, unpaid internships, professional development activities, studying for and taking a certification exam, involvement in professional and/or industry groups, or other training to boost hard skills (welding, precision machining, Excel, Access, QuickBooks, etc.).

In fact, <u>hard skills are so important in this market</u> that there is a separate chapter devoted solely to how you might go about acquiring them.

So, if you don't already have them or if they are not up to date, *go get them now*. And revise your resume, marketing materials, and verbal communication to let the market know that you are in the process of acquiring them. Even a Labrador retriever can get hired if he is a whiz at Excel macros. So why not go get the training?

## Strategy #99
### Send Out a Revised Resume

*Email a revised resume to all your contacts to announce your job search reboot.* Think of it as the comeback kid's grand re-entrance onto the job search scene!

Even if you are only revising 10% of the content on your resume, make sure that some slightly different words stand out. Use the resume emailing to reintroduce yourself, your core strengths, and your value proposition to networking contacts and companies. A resume re-do gets attention. Just make sure the content will knock their socks off.

## Strategy #100
### Demonstrate Your New Approach

*Be involved in activities you weren't before.* Of course, demonstrating that you also have stayed up on best practices content in your profession and industry are also critical. But you need to show the world that you are behaving differently as well. What might this look like? Well, you could:

- Show up for networking or business events.
- Send hand writing thank you notes each day to contacts who helped you out.
- Join and blog on LinkedIn groups.
- Volunteer for community organizations
- Take a course to acquire hard skills (Whoops, did I say that already? Must be important).

## Strategy #101

## Be Your Best Self

*Look, sound, and behave like your best self <u>at all times</u>.* It is up to you to create your own career karma and presenting your "best self" at all times will be key.

Adopt these mantras and keep them front and center at all times:

**Each person's perception is their reality.**

And

**You get one chance to make a first impression.**

So, dressing for success, taking care of personal hygiene, keeping your car clean inside and out, never using angry or foul language, adhering to online etiquette, acting considerate and helpful to others, minding your manners…these are all examples of how you need to present yourself to be perceived as a top candidate by the market.

*Make your own list of daily "best self" must do's and check in with yourself at three or four pre-scheduled times each day to take a brief self-inventory.*

A simple guideline to follow: be comfortable in your own skin but assume there is always someone watching; become a "comfortably confident professional." Does that sound like an oxymoron? Perhaps. But it is exactly what you need to do now.

Of course, the longer you are your "best self," the more you will naturally assume that role…it will become real for you.

So, imagine being yourself, only better. Someone in whom colleagues place greater trust, someone who friends relate to easier, someone who family members *want* to love and respect more.

In other words, since you are going to be putting in the effort regardless, why not let your job search rescue positively impact the rest of your life, as well? Allow your efforts at being your best self to actually become part of the authentic you. Actually *become* your best self.

# Bonus Chapter

## Six Lists of Top 10 Tips

A review of important aspects of the six key parts of a job-search to keep you sharp on the fundamentals.

*"If you are going through hell, keep going."*
- Winston Churchill

Following from the Churchill quote, consider these six quick-hitter lists as tools to help you "keep going" when you are perhaps a bit stressed and in danger of forgetting the fundamentals. The job search areas covered are:

- Revising the Resume
- Applying for a Job
- Daily Job Search
- Networking
- Interviewing
- Negotiating

You could also use these top ten tip lists as checklists. Or modify them with other best job search practices. Just keep believing in yourself and in the value you will bring to your next employer. Don't ever give up, no matter how tough it gets.

You are worth the effort.

## Revising the Resume *Top 10 Tips*

**1. Don't Throw Away the Good Stuff**

Whether you are just tweaking the document or engaged in a total makeover, it's easy to toss out effective wording by mistake. Before making any revisions, go through and highlight your best stuff so you'll be sure to keep it.

**2. Use Adjectives Sparingly**

Especially when trying to power up marketing materials, it is tempting to choose words like "very," "strong," and "excellent." Instead, use words like "proven" and "accomplished."

**3. Make Every Word Count**

Load up with great content and worry less about white space. But don't use "the" and "a" if you don't have to. Additionally, begin bullets with carefully chosen action verbs.

**4. Focus on Accomplishments**

Detailing your accomplishments is easily the #1 priority for writing a powerful resume. Don't hold back on detailing the results you've achieved and how you've achieved them.

**5. Use Numbers Liberally**

The #2 priority for writing a powerful resume is using numerical values, such as: "teamed with 4 co-workers," "saved the company $12K," and "completed the project in 5 months."

### 6. Be Honest and Accurate

A no brainer? Sometimes it's tough when you're trying to remember numbers, for example. Don't omit key information; just err on the side of caution. Write: "completed 60–75 calls per day" or "sold to 15+ new accounts each month."

### 7. Use Bold, Capital Letters, and Italics Sparingly

Carefully choose words and phrases to stand out. Also, ditch the underlines and parentheses.

### 8. Make Your Brand Clearly Stand Out

The 2–3 core strengths that comprise your brand must be plainly evident. You need to use a word megaphone to broadcast your value to the market. Otherwise, your resume-writing will have been a waste of time. Don't be modest.

### 9. Proofread and Edit 'till the Cows Come Home

You should spend almost as much time proofreading and editing as writing. Make sure to read it backwards, too. And, there's no substitute for having another pair of eyes…

### 10. Get Help

Even the Lone Ranger needed a trusty sidekick. So enlist the help of resume-savvy friends who will give you honest feedback and guidance. And, if you have to, call a professional resume writer. Just remember, you usually get what you pay for.

## Applying for a Job *Top 10 Tips*

### 1. Determine a Potential Fit or Don't Apply

Make sure there is a fit with your skills, personality, and ability to get results—that you are able to either take away or prevent the hiring manager's pain. Research and network each best opportunity; apply for five, not 25.

### 2. Network Your Way In

There is no substitute for human contact—in gathering research and getting noticed. Online activity is easier but with more limited value.

### 3. Be Honest and Complete on Applications

This seems basic but is critical. Writing "see resume" means you don't follow directions.

### 4. Customize the Resume with Keywords

Every application needs a customized resume, even if it takes just five minutes. Identify key words/phrases from the job ad and networking. Put them prominently on the resume. Better yet, customize with their 2−3 core hiring motives.

### 5. Identify and Target 2−3 Core Hiring Motives

This is my lingo for applying Pareto's Rule. Know the hiring manager's 2−3 most important requirements, which account for 80% of the job's success. Customize your resume and interview stories to show you are the best candidate to take away or prevent their pain.

### 6. Get Your Resume to the Hiring Manager

This is critical. The ATS/Applicant Tracking System software eats resumes. Use a networking contact, go direct, or employ any means necessary to let the hiring manager know you are interested. Of course, also apply online.

### 7. Be Smart with Cover Letters

Cover letters are usually just not read. Instead, invest time crafting a compelling 3 – 4 line email. If required, use a T-style or other format-style letter that shows you meet the top 2 – 3 hiring motives or most important requirements. The web is full of T-style examples.

### 8. Consider Your List of Professional References

For each application, think tactically about your reference list — who is on it and the order of the names. List 4 – 6 strong work contacts.

### 9. Hold Back on Talking Compensation

He who speaks first loses. Online applications force you to pick a number, but do not give a number or range in dialogue. Too low = you are locked in. Too high = no interview. Instead, say that job "fit" is most important to you.

### 10. Fill Any Gaps

If you are a close match for a certain job but are lacking one skill…go get training for that skill. Even if you are still in training when you apply, it is often enough to get you considered.

## **Daily Job Search** *Top 10 Tips*

### 1. Choose Three Tasks to Accomplish

You may have a lot on your calendar but make sure, every day, you choose the top three items to get done. Do a noon-time check-in with yourself and don't quit until all are crossed off!

### 2. Get Out of the House

Get out of the house every day to boost mood and productivity. It may take gas in the car and time, but plan one networking meeting a day for three days in a row instead of three meetings in one day. No networking meetings? Then head to the library or Starbucks.

### 3. Limit Screen Time

Except for researching, networking, or emailing. Limit yourself to two hours per week of looking for openings. And shut off the phone for hours at a time. The screen is a huge distractor.

### 4. Achieve Self-Care Goals

Schedule at least one self-care mini-goal per day. Whether exercising, eating right, or talking with a friend, don't let yourself down. Include positive self-talk as a mini-goal every day.

### 5. Treat Every Day as a Work Day

Get up early, shower, and dress comfortably but professionally. No t-shirts. Adhere to a pre-planned schedule and breaks. Get the job done.

## 6. Take 5–10 minute Stretch Breaks Every Hour

Your brain will work so much better if you take regular breaks and move around. You may also "schedule" distractions at this time (text, check Facebook, etc.) so they aren't really distractions!

## 7. Schedule in 75% Networking Time

If it isn't scheduled, it won't happen. Up to 80% of all jobs are found via networking and nearly the same percentage of my clients cite networking as key to setting up a strong interview. Also, remember to schedule in regular follow-ups with your contacts.

## 8. Be Kind

Boost your mood by doing something nice for someone else every day. Write a "thank you" card or offer a compliment—keep it simple.

## 9. Focus Efforts on 10+ Target Companies

Have a "rolling" list of target companies and concentrate your daily networking and search activities around them. Even if you don't end up employed at one of these companies, your focused efforts will yield much greater results.

## 10. Use a System to Keep Yourself Accountable

Even the most motivated job seeker will see their effort start to wane after two weeks. Find an "accountability buddy" or create a different system to keep yourself moving forward.

## Networking *Top 10 Tips*

### 1. Be Mobile Integrated

To maximize efficiency, you need to be mobile integrated, with calendars, contacts, and email that all sync with your computer. You need appointment reminders and 24/7 email access.

### 2. Follow Up Every 4–6 Weeks

Networking is less about quantity, more about quality. Develop relationships and ask permission to follow up with each contact 4–6 weeks later. Or risk missing an opportunity.

### 3. Track Progress on a Spreadsheet

Use color codes to rank contact importance, link each contact to a database, and be vigilant about keeping accurate records about dates of contact and your last conversation or e-exchange.

### 4. Make Two New Contacts Each Day

Since you will be following up with contacts made 4–6 weeks ago, making two new contacts per day is manageable and effective. If you miss a day, double up.

### 5. Create Business Cards

You can create professional cards online at vistaprint.com or you can go local. Just don't have perforated edges, please. You may only use a couple cards in your search but don't be without one at a key moment.

### 6. Have One In-Person Meeting Each Day

Whether you are an extrovert or introvert, an in-person meeting will boost your confidence, give you momentum, and force you to practice interpersonal skills also used in interviewing.

### 7. Write Out and Practice an Elevator Pitch

This isn't about monologues. The contents of a 30—60 second intro (your professional history, strengths/value, and job search objective) will be critical to use in two-way dialogue and will force you to be consistent in your messaging.

### 8. Give the Gift of Helping

Remind yourself daily of how good you feel when someone asks you for help. That's how you make those networking contacts feel if you graciously and professionally ask for *their* help.

### 9. Target Hiring Managers

Whether or not you have any bridges to them, you need to network with hiring managers as much as possible. Even if they don't have any openings, their peers might...

### 10. Use LinkedIn and Social Media

Make sure your smiling headshot and profile are ready-for-market, as up to 30% of good paying jobs are now filled with candidates from LinkedIn. LinkedIn is the quickest way to find your former co-workers and contacts at target companies or for you to be found by them!

## Interviewing *Top 10 Tips*

### 1. Be 10–15 Minutes Early

Arriving in the company's parking lot any more than 15 minutes early is desperation. But, when you figure the time it takes to drive there, build in 45 extra minutes in case traffic is re-routed.

### 2. Take Care of Appearance Details

Shined shoes matter. A pressed long-sleeve shirt matters. The inside of your car matters. Of course, if the interview consists of driving a dozer in a gravel pit, lose the tie and put on the steel-toed work boots and clean jeans. If you are unsure of any details, you owe it to yourself to speak with someone who is sure.

### 3. Research Everything

Research position, culture, interviewers. Use the web but also speak with actual people, too. Identify their top 2–3 hiring motives or most important criteria. Pinpoint their pain.

### 4. Keep Your Answers to 30-60 seconds Maximum

Interviews need to be anchored in dialogue. It's OK to have a 10 minute, in-depth discussion about one topic, but don't ever talk straight for more than one minute at a time.

### 5. Have 5–10+ Great Questions Ready

You will be asked if you have any questions. A deafening silence would seal your fate.

### 6. Have 10−15+ Example Stories Prepared

Example stories will highlight achievements and skills, and be aligned with the hiring manager's 2−3 core hiring motives. One or two need to demonstrate your values.

### 7. Be Ready for All Interview Question Types

Be ready for behavioral, situational, and motivation questions. Remember to use your example stories in each answer.

### 8. Pay Attention to Your Non-Verbals

Fact: Your spoken words account for less than 10% of the message you are communicating. The other 90%+ of your message comes from your posture, facial expression, eye contact, use of hands, body motion, and other non-verbals.

### 9. Prepare a Strong Close

You may not be comfortable asking for the job, but you need to offer a firm handshake and make your "high level of interest" known in order to validate their positive impression of your candidacy. Leave nothing on the table.

### 10. Send a Thank You

Hand-written is best if there is time but make sure every interviewer receives a customized email. Reiterate your belief that the position and people seem like a good fit, but don't gush.

## **Negotiating** *Top 10 Tips*

### 1. Do the Research

You can't ask or be the one to bring up compensation but you need to scour the web and speak with contacts to find out any information you can before negotiations begin.

### 2. Don't Speak First

I can't say this too much: <u>he who speaks first loses.</u> They will ask what you want. And you will say it's about "fit" or "challenge" or something. Don't downplay your expectations about being paid competitively but don't talk money until they make an offer. Keep quiet.

### 3. Know Your Bottom Line

Have an idea of what your bottom line is before entering into a dialogue. Otherwise, you can't develop a strategy or understand how to react to their offer.

### 4. Remain Positive and Poised

This is about tone, appropriate silence, and just acting confident. In fact, even if you don't get any more money, an attempt at negotiating shows that you believe in yourself and validates their decision to make you an offer.

### 5. Negotiate Money First

If you have several items to negotiate, either go for it all at once or talk money first.

### 6. Think Win-Win

Don't ever try a scorched-earth strategy. This is not like negotiating for a house or car, where you never have to deal with the seller again. You are about to get "professionally married"

### 7. Believe in Yourself and Your Value

Even if they had other great candidates, they chose you. Be ready to restate your value and do it with conviction, reminding them of the results they will witness with you on the job.

### 8. Make a List of Questions Ahead of Time

Before entering into negotiations, have ready and waiting every question you need answered. It is your right to know details about the benefits plan, workspace, and other factors that might influence your decision.

### 9. Use Open-Ended Statements

Skilled negotiators almost never ask questions, especially those which elicit a "yes" or "no" answer. Use open-ended statements to draw them back to dialogue so they will give up more information and move closer to your position.

### 10. Validate Their Decision with Enthusiasm

Don't act coy. Don't gush with appreciation either. They want to know you agree with their offer decision. Show them enthusiasm and it will strengthen your negotiating position.

# Selected Resources

*The resources in this incomplete list have, over many years, provided fuel for my thought and concept development, to supplement what I have learned from my clients and networking conversations. A number of these books are available in more recent versions than the ones listed here. Each book can be found on my office shelf and I often recommend these titles to clients. This list is intended as much to serve as a resource list starting point for the reader as it is to insure I give credit to some of those who helped inform my own professional development.*

Alessandra, Anthony J., and Michael J. O'Connor. *The Platinum Rule: Discover the Four Basic Business Personalities--and How They Can Lead You to Success*. New York: Warner, 1996.

Beatty, Richard H. *The Five-minute Interview: A Job Hunter's Guide to a Successful Interview*. Hoboken, NJ: John Wiley, 2002.

Bregman, Peter. *18 Minutes: Find Your Focus, Master Distraction, and Get the Right Things Done*. New York: Business Plus, 2011.

Breitbarth, Wayne. *The Power Formula for LinkedIn Success: Kick-start Your Business, Brand, and Job Search*. Austin, TX: Greenleaf Book Group, 2011.

Burka, Jane B., and Lenora M. Yuen. *Procrastination: Why You Do It, What to Do about It*. Reading, MA: Addison Wesley Pub., 1983.

Chapman, Gary D., and Paul E. White. *The 5 Languages of Appreciation in the Workplace: Empowering Organizations by Encouraging People*. Chicago: Northfield Pub., 2011.

Clifton, Jim. *The Coming Jobs War: What Every Leader Must Know about the Future of Job Creation*. New York, NY: Gallup, 2011.

Dawson, Kenneth M., and Sheryl N. Dawson. *Job Search: The Total System*. Hoboken, NJ: Wiley, 1996.

Enelow, Wendy S., and Louise Kursmark. *Expert Resumes for Military-to-civilian Transitions*. Indianapolis, IN: JIST Works, 2010.

Ferrazzi, Keith. *Who's Got Your Back: The Breakthrough Program to Build Deep, Trusting Relationships That Create Success-- and Won't Let You Fail*. New York: Broadway, 2009.

Figler, Howard E., and Richard Nelson. Bolles. *The Career Counselor's Handbook*. Berkeley, CA: Ten Speed, 1999.

Fiore, Neil A. *The Now Habit: A Strategic Program for Overcoming Procrastination and Enjoying Guilt-free Play*. New York: Tarcher/Penguin, 2007.

Fisher, Roger, William Ury, and Bruce Patton. *Getting to Yes: Negotiating Agreement without Giving in*. New York, NY: Penguin, 1991.

Goleman, Daniel. *The Brain and Emotional Intelligence: New Insights*. Northampton, MA: More Than Sound, 2011.

Heath, Chip, and Dan Heath. *Made to Stick: Why Some Ideas Survive and Others Die*. New York: Random House, 2007.

Karrass, Chester Louis. *Give & Take: The Complete Guide to Negotiating Strategies and Tactics*. New York: Crowell, 1974.

Littler, Dale. *The Blackwell Encyclopedia of Management*. Malden, MA: Blackwell Pub., 2005.

Levinson, Jay Conrad., Jeannie Levinson, and Amy Levinson. *Guerrilla Marketing: Easy and Inexpensive Strategies for Making Big Profits from Your Small Business*. Boston, MA: Houghton Mifflin, 2007.

Lucht, John. *Rites of Passage at $100,000 to $1 Million: Your Insider's Lifetime Guide to Executive Job-changing and Faster Career Progress*. New York: Viceroy, 2007

Lynch, Liz. *Smart Networking: Attract a following in Person and Online*. New York: McGraw-Hill, 2009.

Myers, Isabel Briggs., and Peter B. Myers. *Gifts Differing*. Palo Alto, CA: Consulting Psychologists, 1980.

Patterson, Kerry. *Change Anything: The New Science of Personal Success*. New York: Business Plus, 2011.

Shatkin, Laurence. *150 Best Recession-proof Jobs*. Indianapolis, IN: JIST Works, 2009.

Schawbel, Dan. *Me 2.0: 4 Steps to Building Your Future*. New York: Kaplan Pub., 2010.

Sujansky, Joanne Genova., and Jan Ferri-Reed. *Keeping the Millennials: Why Companies Are Losing Billions in Turnover to This Generation--and What to Do about It*. Hoboken, NJ: John Wiley & Sons, 2009.

Tieger, Paul D., and Barbara Barron-Tieger. *Do What You Are: Discover the Perfect Career for You through the Secrets of Personality Type*. New York: Little, Brown, 2007.

Troutman, Kathryn K., and Laura Sachs. Hills. *Ten Steps to a Federal Job: Navigating the Federal Job System, Writing Federal Resumes, KSAs and Cover Letters with a Mission*. Baltimore, MD: Resume Place, 2002.

Watkins, Michael. *The First 90 Days: Proven Strategies for Getting up to Speed Faster and Smarter*. Boston, MA: Harvard Business Review, 2013.

# About the Author

Greg has more than 15 years of experience in career coaching, resume-writing, outplacement and consulting for scores of companies. Previously an executive/retained recruiter, he has helped write thousands of resumes and has trained or coached more than 8,000 individuals in job-search techniques. Greg has also published *You, On Paper: Expert Help on How to Write a Resume*.

Greg has created unique career management concepts and has also done work related to authenticity and masks, capacity and resiliency, locus of control, self-efficacy, and the need for relationship. Greg is informed mainly by humanist thinking, including the work of Carl Rogers, Parker Palmer, and his mother, Marijane Fall.

When not working or traveling, you can find Greg at home in southern Maine with his wife, 2 children, 2 cats, and 1 dog. Greg and his family feel blessed to live near ocean and mountains where they can be active in the outdoors.

Every day Greg practices gratitude and unconditional positive regard. Greg's energy is marked by positivity, genuine caring, forgiveness, and continuous learning.

He can be reached at greg@jobsearchrescue.com